I0879309

On January 7 1943, the German government, in order to free adult soldiers for frontline duty, ordered that all male students of secondary schools born in 1926 and 1927 be drafted into anti-aircraft service in the homeland. Students were to arrive in batteries on February 18 1943. After serving from one year (those born in 1926) to thirteen months (those born in 1927), the boys were transferred into the Reich Labor Service and from there into the armed forces. They were replaced by boys born in 1928 who served to the end of the war. About 200,000 boys became *Flakhelfer*. Most were called up at sixteen, but many, like the author, Karl Heinz Schlesier, were only fifteen. The boys served in batteries of light and heavy flak. Although the government insisted school programs continue for *Flakhelfer*, the effort was a sham, especially where heavy bombing occurred. Schlesier, a student of Rethel *Gymnasium* in Düsseldorf, served as *Flakhelfer* in the regions that suffered the most numerous and heaviest air raids of the war in the Rhineland (Düsseldorf) and the Ruhr (Recklinghausen). His is a coming of age story in a world gone mad, where a teenage boy launched shrapnel into a sky filled with bombers, where Christmas-tree-like flares marked cities about to burn, where working beside Russian POWs, protecting industries with slave labor, courting a girl among bombed-out ruins, and spending leave with family hiding in claustrophobic bomb shelters was unremarkable, as was finally being thrown, unprepared, into a disintegrating frontline only fifty kilometers from his childhood home. The memoir is based solely on Schlesier's diary notes and memories of that period. He has consciously avoided including what he learned after the war. His views, opinions, and interpretations of events are from inside the Germany of that time. If some are inconvenient today, they mirror the chaos of the world he experienced. Then, to live or not to live was accidental. Schlesier wrote this memoir as an old man in response to a granddaughter's question about what he did in the war. This is his answer. Perhaps, he also gives a voice to the silent generation of boys born in Germany in 1926 and 1927. This generation has been silent because the horror it knew pales in comparison to the horror of the Holocaust.

Karl Heinz Schlesier was born in Düsseldorf, Germany on July 31 1927. Following the experiences in this memoir, he attended Bonn University studying anthropology and art history. His Ph.D. described the art of the pre-Inca Nazca of Peru. A post-doctoral fellowship at the University of Chicago in 1958 introduced him to Sol Tax and action anthropology. Action anthropology was designed to benefit host populations. Schlesier began working with the Cheyenne in Oklahoma in 1968. Ever since, he has supported Cheyenne traditional leadership in their struggle to retain important features of their ancient culture and adapt them to the realities of the present and future.

The author is best known for his work with and writings about American Indians. Of his eight books, six deal with Indian issues, as do most of his many articles in the scholarly journals of eleven countries. His books include the award winning novels *Trail of the Red Butterfly* and *Aurora Crossing*, as well as *Josanie's War* and *Plains Indians, A.D.500-1500*. Schlesier served as a Jury Member on the Fourth Russell Tribunal, "The Rights of the Indians of the Americas," Rotterdam, 1980, and twice as expert witness on Cheyenne cases in Federal Court in Oklahoma City.

Flakhelfer to Grenadier

Memoir of a Boy Soldier, 1943-1945

Karl H. Schlesier

Helion & Company

Helion & Company Limited
26 Willow Road
Solihull
West Midlands
B91 1UE
England
Tel. 0121 705 3393
Fax 0121 711 4075
Email: info@helion.co.uk
Website: www.helion.co.uk
Twitter: @helionbooks
Visit our blog http://blog.helion.co.uk/

Published by Helion & Company 2014
Designed and typeset by Bookcraft Ltd, Stroud, Gloucestershire
Cover designed by Paul Hewitt, Battlefield Design (www.battlefield-design.co.uk)
Printed by Lightning Source Ltd, Milton Keynes, Buckinghamshire

Text and images © Karl H. Schlesier
Cover: Author on the gunner's seat. *4. Zug*, Hüls, spring 1944 (author's collection).

ISBN 978 1 909384 98 9

British Library Cataloguing-in-Publication Data.
A catalogue record for this book is available from the British Library.

All rights reserved. No part of this publication may be reproduced, stored in a retrieval system,or transmitted, in any form, or by any means, electronic, mechanical, photocopying, recording or otherwise, without the express written consent of Helion & Company Limited.

For details of other military history titles published by Helion & Company Limited contact the above address, or visit our website: http://www.helion.co.uk.

We always welcome receiving book proposals from prospective authors.

In memory of my parents

Wär da ein Got
und im Fleisch,
und könnte mich rufen, ich würd
umhergehen, ich würd
warten ein wenig.

Johannes Bobrowki, Immer zu Benennen.
Aus: *Sarmatische Zeit, Schattenland Ströme*, Deutsche Verlagsanstalt,
Stuttgart 1961, 1962.

Were there a God,
and in flesh,
and could call me, I would
walk around, I would
wait a little.

Contents

Glossary

Abgedeckt	'Covered' – readiness call made by the gunners when the command pointer of the dials in front of them was covered with the position pointer.
Abteilung	Battalion/detachment.
Christbäume	Red and green flares dropped by Pathfinder planes to mark the area of the bomb drop.
Dicke Autos	"Fat cars," gunner slang for four-engined bombers.
Flieger HJ	Branch of the Hitler Youth associated with the *Luftwaffe*.
Commando-Gerät 40	Command Device 40, the standard fire-control predictor in the flak arm.
Fähnrich	Officer-candidate.
Feldpolizei	Field police.
Flakkampfabzeichen	Flak combat badge.
Funktions-Schiessen	Test-firing the light flak guns during a night alarm, usually once a month.
(Focke Wulf) Fw 190	German fighter plane.
Gebirgsjäger	Member of a German Mountain Division.
Geschütz-Staffel	Gun personnel.
Grosskampfbatterie	An enlarged heavy Flak battery composed of two regular batteries with six artillery pieces each.
Gruppenfeuer	Each gun of the battery firing at the same moment.
Heer	Army.
Hiwi	*Hilfswillige*, a Russian prisoner of war who had volunteered to serve in the German anti-aircraft arm.
Kaserne	Barracks.
Kinderlandverschickung (KLV)	The mass evacuation of school children from urban areas under repeated air attacks to distant rural areas.
Kreuzlafette	The four extensions of the gun carriage affixed crosswise to the ground.
Kübelwagen	Standard light passenger cross-country car (4x4) used by the German armed forces, in size slightly larger than a Jeep.
Lagerführer	Person charged with maintaining discipline in a camp.
Luftschutz	Air raid defense corps.
Mattscheibe	Searchlights pointed straight up and remaining stationary, aimed at a heavy cloud cover.
(Messerschmitt) Me 109	German fighter plane.
Mess-Staffel	Fire-control post personnel.
MG 42	Machine-gun 42, with a rate of fire of 1200 rounds per minute, entered service in 1942.

Panzerfaust — The *Panzerfaust* was a recoilless disposable lightweight one-man antitank weapon firing a large hollow-charge grenade. Later models increased the range from 30 to 100 meters, the armour penetration from 140 mm at 30° to 200mm at 30°. A portion of the gases from the propellant charge in the disposable firing tube vented to the rear to eliminate recoil. These made conspicuous the firing position of the operator and created a danger zone behind the *Panzerfaust.*

Pulk — Group of bombers, usually twenty to thirty, flying in a close formation, also called a "box".

Reichsarbeitsdienst (*RAD*) — Reich Labor Service, as initiated by the Nazi government, was a nine-month period of service for 18-19 year olds, both male and female, prior to the inductment of the males into the armed services. By 1944 the period of service had been reduced to twelve weeks, devoted mostly to basic military training.

StuG III — *Sturmgeschütz III*, assault gun.

Sturmgewehr — Assault rifle, also referred to as the MP43 or MP44. Heavily influential in the development of Mikhail Kalashnikov's AK-47.

Tross-Staffel — Supply personnel.

Vierling — Quadruple-barreled flak cannon.

Viermot — "Four engines", gunner slang for four-engine Allied bomber.

Wehrbezirkskommando — District recruiting office for the *Wehrmacht.*

Wehrmacht — Armed forces.

Wirbelwind — Anti-aircraft tank, featuring a quadruple-barrelled 2cm gun on a converted Panzer IV chassis.

Zug — Section.

Preface

On January 7 1943 the German government, in order to free adult soldiers for frontline duty, ordered, all male students of elite secondary schools (*Gymnasium*, *Oberrealschule*) born in 1926 and 1927 to be drafted into anti-aircraft service in the homeland. A government decree on January 22 1943 informed the schools fourteen days in advance of February 15 1943, the date of the call-up, the day the students were ordered to arrive at their designated batteries. The official term for them was *Luftwaffenhelfer* (Air Force Auxiliaries) although they were more often, and more correctly, called *Flakhelfer* (Anti-Aircraft Auxiliaries); the word is both singular and plural.

Boys born in 1926 served in the batteries until February 1944, when they were transferred into the *Reichsarbeitsdienst* (Reich Labor Service) and from there into the *Heer*. They were replaced by boys born in 1927 from another branch of schools of secondary education in the German system: trade schools and middle schools. All those born in 1927 served until September 9 1944, when they were transferred into the *Reichsarbeitsdienst* and from there into the *Heer*. Boys born in 1928, both from elite secondary schools and trade and middle schools, replaced the *Flakhelfer* of the 1927 lot and served from September 1944 to the end of the war on May 9 1945.

A total of approximately 200,000 boys served as *Flakhelfer*. Their average age was sixteen, but due to their date of birth quite a few were still fifteen when they were called up. Although they came to see themselves as soldiers, and were usually regarded as such by their adult comrades, the government defined them as students doing soldiers' work. Since they could not leave the batteries to go to school, school went to them. Male teachers beyond draft age were summoned to continue the boys' education in an environment not conducive to learning the traditional fare of secondary schools. The government was most concerned about the education of the *Flakhelfer* from *Gymnasium* and *Oberrealschule* and demanded a weekly program of instruction for these to include 4 hours of German literature, 3 hours of history, 4 hours of Latin. 3 hours of mathematics, 2 hours of physics, and 2 hours of chemistry. It is obvious that the program was doomed to fall far short of its goal, especially in areas were heavy bombing had to be met by increased anti-aircraft activity, e.g., the Ruhr region and the Rhineland. With the known world around them falling into shambles, *Flakhelfer* were hard pressed not to see the whole effort as a sham.

In the batteries in which they served, in the light flak (2cm and 3.7cm guns) and heavy flak (8.8cm, 10.5cm and 12.8cm guns), the boys wore dark-grey *Luftwaffe* fatigues. The dress uniform, as ordered by the government, was tunic, ski pants and ski cap in the blue cloth of the *Flieger HJ*, the branch of the Hitler Youth associated with the *Luftwaffe*. This uniform had a removable swastika armband on the upper left arm. Many resented the armband and took it off during furlough whenever possible. Generally, battery chiefs were tolerant in this matter and did not enforce a dress code they saw as superfluous; they had more serious concerns. Also, most were genuinely fond of "their" boys and protected them when possible.

The constantly growing inferno of the air war took a toll on anti-aircraft batteries protecting industrial and military installations and open German cities. The first *Flakhelfer* to become casualties were six who died at their guns in an air raid on Berlin, March 1 1943, fourteen days after they had been recruited. Many *Flakhelfer* became engaged in ground combat when their batteries and the cities they protected were overrun by Allied armies in the West and East. Many, like their adult comrades, became prisoners of war and spent many months in Allied prisoner of war camps.

I was one of them. This is the memoir of one *Flakhelfer*, a road traveled by countless others, en route to a short, violent career as a Grenadier. Going back into one's personal past requires an unshakable, shameless commitment to truth. It is a scout's search through dark and foreboding territory once known but veiled by the mind's effort to block memories to preserve sanity. Whether the scout's journey was worth the strain and distress must be decided by others. Rarely is the past a fun place to visit.

Views, opinions and interpretations of situations and events expressed here are those from inside Germany during the years 1943 to 1945. They are unaltered by post- war insights and uninfluenced by objective historical scholarship. They are inconvenient today but mirror the chaos of the time and place. Then, whether one lived or not was accidental.

All characters, names and places mentioned here are factual. Names of my buddies in Reisholz and Hüls are nicknames we used among ourselves; mine was Kalla. The complete names are these: Ferdi, Ferdinand Bleines; Thei, Rolf Thiemann; Hannes, Hans Nolden; Wenner, Bernhard Wenzel; Bergittimus, Horst Bergfeld. Of the old crew, I must thank Ferdi, in Köln, for our spirited discussions when I was writing this book.

I must step away from the memoir for a moment. Readers might find it difficult to accept that it contains little mention of German war crimes, especially the organized mass murder of Jews and Gypsies. In the narrow mental space in which a fifteen- to sixteen- year old *Flakhelfer* and a seventeen-year old Grenadier was forced to live, and in the narrow mental space in which most families in Germany were forced to live, there existed no information about the crimes the SS and, sometimes, German military units, were committing elsewhere. This may be hard to fathom. But the Nazi state had obliterated all democratic institutions of post-World War I Germany, including the free press, trade unions, political parties and the judiciary. Universities had been reduced to trade schools from which all personnel had been evicted who did not follow the party line. A cloud of oppression had descended upon Germany. The State permitted only what the state regarded as essential for its own survival. Every independent voice had been hushed. Those who knew something of these horrors and spoke up faced severe punishment or death. Sources outside the country who were aware of the magnitude of Nazi crimes either kept silent as, for instance, the Vatican and the German Catholic hierarchy, from cardinals to bishops to the local clergy, or their voices did not reach into Germany. Even if they had, Nazi control was so complete that it would not have made a difference. And there was a war going on, with husbands and sons on distant battlefields or already dead or crippled. The population, shocked by the hammer blows of the Allied bomber campaign, was not capable of considering German misdeeds, had it known about them, or of revolting even for its own sake. Truth is that under these conditions the great majority of Germans only learned after the war what terrible crimes had been perpetrated in their name. Recognition of the facts was instrumental in the constitution and the emergence of a new post-war German democracy that thoroughly separated itself from the dark twelve-year episode of the Hitler and SS years. Still, three generations after the German bid for dominance and the Holocaust, Germans acknowledge a burden of shame for what was once done in the German name.

Acknowledgements

Special thanks are due to my patient, encouraging wife, Claire, my first reader, and to my generous, thoughtful writer-friend, J. M. Hayes, my first editor.

Prologue

SEPTEMBER 9 1958.

On a balmy, sunny morning, I made my first visit to downtown Chicago. I had arrived a few days earlier from Germany to continue graduate studies in anthropology at the University of Chicago on a post-doctoral fellowship. Making my way into the Loop I was awed by the spectacle of the great city, the packed traffic, the bustling crowds, the huge, shiny, unmarred buildings, so different from the battle-scarred cities of my homeland. In the middle of Michigan Avenue stood a blue-uniformed city cop directing traffic.

I readied my camera to take a picture to memorize the day, the beginning of something new in a world as yet unknown to me. The cop eyed me briefly as I approached him and snapped a shot. Without taking his eyes off the traffic he waved me to his side. Tall, slender, with an attentive face, he was a few years older than I. When I stood next to him, he quickly looked me over and asked, "Where are you from?"

"Germany," I said.

"Where in Germany?"

"Düsseldorf."

He nodded and looked at me directly. "I bombed Düsseldorf." It was a blunt statement of fact. There was neither regret nor satisfaction in his voice.

Taken aback, I blurted out, "I was an anti-aircraft gunner in "Düsseldorf." He smiled. Suddenly we were two survivors who had once experienced dread at the same place. Bending close to me, he said, "Isn't it great to be alive?"

1
Going Home

Leaving, June 7, 1943. At 7 o'clock in the morning, as on every morning over the past five months, we stood in ranks on the open square between the buildings. We stood at attention as the flag with the swastika was raised.

We were 38 boys of Rethel *Gymnasium* in Düsseldorf. Most of us were fifteen years old, a few were sixteen. I was fifteen. A boy a year older from our school stood at the head of the three-ranks formation. He was the *Lagerführer*, charged with keeping discipline in our camp. In front stood the teacher who also served as the director of the camp, the chief. We watched as he saluted the flag when the cloth crept upward on the flagpole and billowed out under a brisk wind from the north.

This was our last day in Bad Einsiedel, a spartan, weathered old spa on the main ridge of the Erzgebirge (Ore Mountains) in southern Saxony, a few stone throws away from the Czech border. Since early February 1943, and for a second time in two years, we had participated in the *Kinderlandverschickung* (KLV), the mass evacuation of many thousands of school children from western cities suffering from Allied air raids to rural areas in eastern Germany. For five months Bad Einsiedel had been our home far away from the raging war. We had lived in isolation, without neighbors, in the great silence of the forests surrounding us, a world that seemed unreal in the calm eye of a violent storm. Our only connection with the outside were letters from home that sometimes included newspaper clippings, usually with bad news, and packages with cakes and cookies and books sent by worried mothers. The delicacies were widely shared among us. The long- awaited order to return to Düsseldorf had arrived a few days earlier.

When the flag-raising ceremony was over we were dismissed and headed to the dining room. The mood was subdued at breakfast that morning. Gone was the friendly noise, the ribbing and the laughter that usually accompanied meals. We ate in silence. We were given extra rations for the journey home. As I walked out I cast a long look back over the dining room the place that had also been our classroom during the day and our meeting room on many evenings. We went to our rooms and fetched our gear, already packed. We carried it downstairs and gathered on the open square, waiting for the trucks that would take us 50 kilometers to the city of Chemnitz, the railroad, and a special train.

Bad Einsiedel, built in the late 19th century, lay in the middle of two long meadows extending north and west. All around were huge, dense forests of mixed leaf and needle trees that held red deer, roe deer, wild boar, and an occasional lynx. Game was numerous; hunting had ended because of the war. The open square was surrounded on three sides by buildings with thick, white-painted walls and wide, overhanging roofs. To the north, in the center, stood the two-story cookhouse with an adjoining dining room and the quarters of the chief and the kitchen and maintenance personnel. To the east, was the one-story barn for two draft horses. To the west, the two-story guest house with guest rooms, our sleeping and living quarters on the second floor, washrooms and utility rooms on the first floor. Behind the dining room lay the bath house over the hot springs that once had made Einsiedel a spa.

It had been an untroubled place for us although we fretted sometimes about relatives in the war and our families, endangered in Düsseldorf. It had come as a shock to us when we heard that the *Afrika-Korps* had surrendered in Tunisia in May. It was a second major disaster, following on Stalingrad three months earlier. Still, as long as the snow lasted we skied and sledded. In the spring we hiked in the forest, watching for game, and on some evenings we played soccer on the meadow below the bath house. The man who doubled as our single teacher and chief of the KLV camp, Dr. Koetter, a bachelor in his late fifties, had been educated at Harrow School in England and had taught us the Harrow Football Song. Sometimes, when we walked to our soccer field, for fun we burst into "Forty years on when afar and a thunder… "

Compared to an earlier KLV camp we had attended in 1942, located in the Riesengebirge in southern Silesia, Einsiedel was a pretty enlightened and relaxed camp. The only concession to demands made by the government was the flag-raising ceremony in the morning. Formal events that required us to wear the regular *Jungvolk* uniform were rare. We usually wore civilian clothes. We were grateful for the informal and free atmosphere.

School had been easy and creative. Because our teacher was certified to teach German Literature, English, and Sports, we missed instruction in Latin, the natural sciences, and another foreign language that would have been in our *gymnasium* program in normal times. In April and May, under his direction, we prepared a stage version of selected parts of Shakespeare's *Julius Caesar*, in German, fashioning the props ourselves. Women from the kitchen staff helped us make the costumes. When we were ready, after a couple of rehearsals, we performed Shakespeare before a select audience, the kitchen and maintenance personnel and the local forester and his family. I suspect we had more fun than the spectators. I was too shy to try for one of the more prominent roles. Instead, because everyone had to be in it, I portrayed a senator in the group of Brutus and Cassius before the knifing. I spoke only a few lines. In another scene I was a Roman soldier, expected to look fierce in his armament, but mute.

School had been held weekday mornings between breakfast and lunch. Afternoon, after homework, we had much time to read, socialize, play games or hike in the woods. There was a good library next to the dining room and I made much use of it. In the evenings we often met in the dining room. Chairs were placed in a circle and we listened to readings of poetry and short stories in German and English followed by discussions. Two weeks before our departure we had begun to read in class, in the original with roles assigned to different readers in every session, the World War I play *Journey's End*, by R.C. Sherriff. We were in our fifth year of English in Bad Einsiedel and had an extended English class every weekday. Each of us owned a copy of the play. We were not able to finish it.

When the trucks arrived on that last morning we said goodbye to the personnel, four middle-aged women and two old men. The chief cook, a heavy-set, warm and friendly woman, was crying. Some of us tried to make jokes to take the sting out of our farewell. The rest of us stood rather frozen, hiding emotions. These people had done well by us. We knew what we had had in Einsiedel. We did not know, anymore, what we would go back to. Letters from our parents had attempted to be reassuring, but we had learned to read between the lines. The general news was disheartening. Cities in the Ruhr area and the Rhineland were under repeated air attacks. When the trucks spun away we were certain that we would never see this place again.

There were three trucks, more than seemed necessary to move us. But these could only be lightly loaded because they were running on wood gas, not gasoline. Each truck had a steel boiler fitted to the hood next to the cabin, a cylindrical device that burned wood and supplied the gas produced in the process to a motor modified to take it. Gasoline was reserved for the military. Its civilian use was severely restricted. As long as the trucks ran on level ground and downhill the ride was smooth. We made the little town of Olbernhau without difficulty. But past Olbernhau the road occasionally climbed rises and low hills. Then the motors sputtered and moaned and slowed down, gaining speed only on downhill stretches. It was clear, sunny day and we watched as we passed isolated farms and sawmills. We cruised through villages nestled into grassy slopes and green forests. It was a ponderous but peaceful journey through charming scenery. It took us three hours on a winding road to get to Chemnitz and the railroad station. We disembarked and settled with our gear on the designated platform.

Our group was not the first to arrive. A boys' camp from Lessing *Gymnasium* in Düsseldorf was already waiting. In the course of the next hour two more KLV classes arrived, one from Scharnhorst *Gymnasium* of our city and one of a girls' *gymnasium* from Neuss, a city across the Rhine southwest of Düsseldorf. The four camps filled the platform. While the chiefs of the camps stood together in a little circle, chatting, we and the other kids sat in four tight clusters, each separate from the others, each confined to itself. Each, over time, had become its own small, closed world of comradeship not shared with outsiders. Although three of the camps on the platform came from the same city and would experience a similar future, we had nothing to say to each other.

It was the same with the girls from Neuss. We registered their presence, having hardly seen a girl during our time in Bad Einsiedel, but our minds that day were on matters other than girls. We sat in a glum mood, barely talking, waiting for the special train to take us home.

We knew that our close-knit group would split up when we arrived in Düsseldorf. Those of us born in 1928 would go back to school on a rotating schedule with another school. Our old school, Rethel, had been destroyed by British bombing in 1942. Before we went to Bad Einsiedel in early February 1943, we had shared in the facilities of a girls' *gymnasium*, Augusta Victoria, a school only lightly damaged. When the girls had school in the morning, we used the rooms in the afternoon. The schedule was reversed every week.

Boys born in 1927 would be drafted into anti-aircraft service as *Flakhelfer*, officially called *Luftwaffenhelfer* (LWH). We knew that draft notices were waiting at home. Eleven of us would go into the flak batteries, me included. This weighed on our minds. We were thinking of our imminent separation.

The train arrived around noon. It had been put together in Dresden and half of its passenger cars were already filled with children being returned to the West. Two cars had been reserved for the groups waiting in Chemnitz. We climbed aboard and sat closely packed in compartments as the engine whistled and puffed smoke and the train departed. The first stop was in Gera, a town 75 kilometers west of Chemnitz. Boys and girls of five more KLV camps climbed in, and the train rolled on through Weimar to Erfurt to pick up another batch of children. As soon as they were loaded, the train continued under a late afternoon sun. It did not stop until we reached Bad Hersfeld in the evening. Here the last empty cars were filled, and the train moved through the night toward its destination, 400 kilometers farther west.

At railroad stations that day, we had seen soldiers on furlough preparing to leave, surrounded by family members saying emotional goodbyes. A couple of times we had been passed by military trains going east, two with tanks and trucks on flatbed cars. In spite of the canvas covers we had identified the freight. Once our train had been halted and placed on a sidetrack to let a train with a more urgent purpose pass. This was a long hospital train, its cars painted with red crosses.

I woke up when our train came to a halt. Looking through the window I noted that the sign under the station roof read Giessen. We waited in the train for four hours, then started moving at dawn. By the time we reached Siegen all of us were awake. Here the train halted again for an hour or more, letting other trains pass in both directions, military and freight trains among them. We were not allowed to leave the train but walked freely about our car, visiting other compartments. Our mood had shifted. We were going home and were getting closer. We were getting excited. We dug into our food rations. We imagined seeing our parents again and others we had left behind, eager for places that meant much to us, the places where we had grown up.

When the train started again, we continued northwest toward Hagen, a city located on the southeast edge of the Ruhr industrial center, a mere 50 kilometers east of Düsseldorf. We crowded the windows and looked into the land of low, forest-covered hills, green and yellow fields, farms, the neat villages and scrubbed little towns of Westphalia. So far, on this rail trip, we had not seen evidence of damage done by the war. It seemed the Allied air offensive concentrated on targets elsewhere.

At noon, close to Hagen, the train once more came to a halt in the little town of Altena. The platform was crowded with people. Whole families, with the young and old, were sitting between packs and bundles looking tired and despondent. Our good feelings died quickly. We had seen this before. These people were refugees from some catastrophe and were being evacuated. What had happened? Where? We watched, concerned. We saw the KLV chiefs and railroad men of our train gather around some officials. A serious discussion appeared to take place. When the meeting broke up, the chiefs returned slowly to the train. We wondered what was going on. Dr. Koetter called our group together. We stood in the narrow space of the clogged aisle. His face was solemn.

"*Jungens,* I have bad news," he said. He paused, looking at us. "Wuppertal was bombed nine days ago, Essen and Dortmund a few days earlier. "

He swallowed. "A lot of people are being evacuated. Our train was supposed to go through Wuppertal but the station master here and authorities are not sure whether we can. They said that the center of the city was destroyed, including the railroad station. They don't know whether the tracks have been repaired yet." His voice faltered. "They will find out."

He looked out the window and back at us. "There is more bad news. Düsseldorf was hit again, twelve nights ago, but not as bad as Wuppertal."

He shook his head. "I'll let you know what I learn." He turned away and shuffled off.

We slowly went back to our seats. We did not look at each other and no one spoke a word. We sat like that until he came back and went from compartment to compartment. When he came to us he put his head through the door and simply said, "We have been cleared. We are going through Wuppertal."

The locomotive slowly began to move. After we covered the short distance to Hagen the train was switched to another track and continued without delay toward Wuppertal. We went through the valley of the Wupper River, a small stream running through a narrow strip of flat ground between steep, slanted slopes dropping down from plateaus above. As we neared Wuppertal-Barmen we saw fire-blackened façades and remnants of walls and cracked chimneys standing around collapsed interiors of houses and buildings – block after block, street after street, lying in ruin. The train moved slowly through a kilometer or more of mounds of broken stones on both sides of the tracks along the walled-in river. Islands, scarred buildings still standing, had survived the inferno when everything else seemed to have perished. It was hard to imagine that any living thing could have survived. But we saw a host of people working in this devastation. Civilians and men in army and firefighters' uniforms, along with women and older men and youths, cleared passages through the rubble. The reeking smell of dead fires still hung in the air. Seeing this numbed us. Once the train stopped briefly, then went past a caved-in railway station and continued on.

We spoke little after that. We were more eager than ever to get home. Now the train rattered down from the Bergische Land, the hill country east of Düsseldorf. Past the Neandertal and Gerresheim, the easternmost suburb of the city, the train slowly reached the large central station badly battered in earlier raids. It was the end of the line for us in late afternoon.

We disembarked quietly. We did not say good-bye to each other, we just separated, each hurrying on his way. On the train there had been KLV classes from Neuss, Mülheim, Duisburg and Mönchen -Gladbach, too. They needed train connections to their cities and blocked every platform of the station. With two of my classmates, Ferdi and Thei, I walked through the main exit to the wide square in front once surrounded by tall, elegant hotels. They were burned-out ruins now. We waited and took the crowded streetcar 9 to Grafenberg. I watched passively as we passed through Flingern, the suburb directly to the east of the heart of the city. Previous raids had taken a toll. Among demolished houses were others, pocked by bomb fragments but intact. The Grafenberger Alley had been fortunate. I saw no recent damage. At Burgmüller Strasse, end of the run of 9, we got off and waited for streetcar 3 to take us to Gerresheim. It came and we climbed aboard. It made the long climb through the woods to the Hardt and the slow descent into upper Gerresheim, where Thei left. Blackened ruins, here and there. Not many. The center of the Old Town of Gerresheim around the 13th century basilica had suffered. But these were wounds from past raids. The streetcar stopped on Dörpfeld Strasse. Ferdi and I got off and walked, he one house down, I a little farther, past the ruins of our neighbor's house. I came to the wide wooden gate. A load lifted from my shoulders. I passed under the tall trees and went up the few stairs to the large metal- covered door. I rang the bell. Everything looked as it had when I left it.

Home Again. My mother was at the door on our second-floor apartment. Her face broke into a wide smile when she recognized me. I felt a bit awkward as she gave me a long, emotional embrace. I had not experienced such affection for quite some time. My father came into the hall. His usually stern face relaxed and he smiled. A short hug, a deft handshake. I knew both so well and knew how much they loved me, but I felt distant. I had become accustomed to the constant company of other boys. I had learned to be solely responsible for myself. At least that is what I thought. It seemed that my ties to my buddies had become stronger than to my parents. I had to remember the bond between us and relearn our relationship.

I carried my gear into my room. I glanced through the tall window that faced the street. Through the old trees, it was possible to glimpse the forested hills less than a kilometer away to the east. The room felt strange to me. Opposite the bookshelves was the .22 rifle on the wall below crossed dueling swords, the latter a gift from a distant relative who claimed he had once used them. Perhaps it was me who had changed. I felt the same when I sat with my parents in the large living room.

They were both in their late forties, my father a year older than my mother. My mother was the same as I remembered her, a sensitive, friendly, outgoing person with dark curly hair, a quick laugh. She often sang in the house while working. My father, an introvert with a serious, sometimes austere manner, looked older than I remembered. What was happening everywhere wore heavily on his mind.

My parents had expected me a day or two earlier and had worried greatly about me. I was only able to make small talk. When I told them about the delay in our travel and mentioned Wuppertal-Barmen, my father's face darkened.

"Wuppertal," he said. "The newspaper reported that about 4,000 people were killed and 130,000 lost their homes." He paused. "There are still bodies under the wreckage that haven't been found. The British used incendiary bombs and air mines. The air mines had a terrible effect in the close space between the heights." He looked at the table top before him. "Düsseldorf was hit during the night of May 25. The area around the zoo was destroyed. Many houses, the skating rink and the zoo are gone. Few of the animals survived." He said it with deep resignation.

"The zoo?" I asked. This was a shock. I had happy memories of the zoo and the skating rink. I had often visited the zoo with my parents when I was little. We boys from Rethel *Gymnasium* had gone to the skating rink in winters past after school, before the British air raids became serious. We went to play ice hockey and skated circles around girls in short skirts – an activity that seemed rather childish thinking about it now. But worst of all, the parents of some of my friends from school lived in upscale neighborhoods around the zoo. What had happened to them? We had heard nothing about this in Bad Einsiedel. Were they all right?

We sat in distressed silence. Finally my father said, "There is an official letter to you from the *Wehrbezirkskommando*. Because you were not here we opened it." He cleared his throat. "You have been drafted as *Flakhelfer*. You have to report to a battery in Reisholz, *4. Schwere Flakabteilung 177/0*." He was a veteran of the First World War and had lived through trench warfare of the worst kind on the Western Front, a trauma for all who had been there. He knew all about war. Now war again closed in on everything and everyone.

I was still ignorant. Passing through Wuppertal-Barmen had been a heavy blow, but it did not last long. It added, however, to a mood, a feeling that what was happening was inevitable, beyond anyone's power to change.

The letter of induction was no surprise to my parents and me. We wondered why it had come so late. My father knew that the son of a colleague in the factory had been drafted on February 25. By that time our group was already in Einsiedel.

Perhaps, other members of my age group were in other KLV camps. It seemed we had slipped by, escaped for a little while.

My parents were grateful that I had been far from danger for a little longer, I was their only child. I always wanted a sister when I was younger, but it could not be. Now they had to give me up again, this time for something dangerous. My mother was clearly afraid for me. My father must have been, too, but he did not show it. I felt uncertain. Some of the kids I knew had already gone to the guns, or would be going soon. Nothing could change that. In some ways, I was looking forward to being with my friends.

The draft letter gave June 3 as the date for reporting to the Reisholz battery. It meant I was already six days overdue. I would have to explain why I was late. I told my parents I would see whether Ferdi, whose parents lived two houses away, had a letter like mine and whether he was ordered to the same battery. My parents remained at the living room as I went to Ferdi's place. His letter was identical to mine. We decided we would report to Reisholz two days from then, on June 10, a Thursday. We would go together.

My parents accepted it as something impossible to change. They knew I would be in trouble if I stayed longer. My mother said sadly, "In five days is Whitsun. We had hoped we would be together. After all this time ..." She did not finish the sentence. She got up and went to the kitchen to prepare supper.

My father and I stayed. Our conversation was hesitant, certainly on my part. We had to learn to know each other again. He asked me about Bad Einsiedel. I said something general. My heart was not in it. We had other things on our minds.

He told me about the situation in the factory. Before the war he had had 50 men under his supervision. Now his workers were a few German men beyond draft age, a handful of forced laborers from Czechoslovakia, and French and Russian prisoners of war. It was difficult for him to get along with this odd bunch. The foreigners were understandably less than enthusiastic about their work. The German workers caused friction when they tried to boss the foreigners around. The Germans complained that the foreigners were treated too well. My father let them know that he treated everyone according to their performance, not according to nationality. This stance was not in accord with the ideas of the Nazi authorities. Unofficially, he had the support of the factory administration. Nevertheless, I understood that he walked a fine line.

My mother called and we went to the dining room. The table was set with care. A white tablecloth, a crystal vase with fresh flowers from the garden. My mother had used our best china, silverware, and crystal glasses for the mineral water. Supper was simple and not much different from pre-war times: a boiled egg, dark bread and sausages. We had a bowl of canned *mirabellen* – yellow plums – from our own trees for dessert, last year's harvest.

My mother offered a short prayer of thanks for the food and my safe return. She always started meals with a prayer. After supper I helped clean the table. When my mother had done the dishes we sat again in the living room. My father carefully loaded his pipe and lit it. He was a light smoker, and the tin of pipe tobacco and the few packs of cigarettes allowed on the monthly ration card were enough for him. For a little while, as the three of us sat together, it seemed like earlier, happier times. But when my parents began to speak about their world we were quickly reminded where we were.

One of my cousins, Willi, had been killed in action in Russia. Another cousin, Paul, was a lieutenant in a *Gebirgsjäger* Division in Italy. I had been at his wedding in Gerresheim in 1942. A third cousin, Walter, was in the Navy somewhere, his whereabouts unknown. My parents spoke haltingly about night alarms, hours spent in the cellar, the rumble of heavy anti-aircraft fire, sometimes the dull concussion of bombs exploding. They lived in constant fear of the house being hit, worrying whether the basement ceiling would hold up. A fear of fire from incendiary bombs. Would they be able to get out or would the cellar become a tomb?

I had experienced some of this before Einsiedel, but the memories had faded there, in the quiet, undisturbed splendor of the forests. It was obvious that everything had gotten worse in my brief absence. The air raids had accelerated, becoming much more devastating than earlier. Newspapers described British bombing, after March 1943 of cities like Essen, Stettin, Köln, Bochum, Dortmund and, recently, Wuppertal-Barmen, as "one thousand bomber raids."

We changed subjects and talked about more pleasant things. My parents wanted to show me the garden, so we went downstairs, through the court edged by the north wall of the house on one side and on the other by the structure that included the wash house, the garage, and the pigeon tower. A few stairs, and we were on the garden's level. It was a productive garden with one morello cherry tree, a large pear tree, two small apple trees, three medium-sized mirabelle trees, berry bushes and the potato, onion and carrot patches omnipresent in German vegetable gardens. The garden supplied a valuable addition to food bought in stores on ration cards. There were also flower beds and, on a long metal frame my father had built over the walkway cutting through the middle of the garden, vine boughs and shoots hung thick with curled leaves and green grapes. When ripe, the grapes were small and sour, and the birds, uncontested, got almost all of them.

The garden was set apart from the wide, fenced park that surrounded the house on three sides and, on the west, extended for 500 meters to a rise crowned by a ruined tower that looked like a castle keep over the Torfbruch Valley toward the city, a few kilometers away. A twelve-cornered part of the tower's cellar was exposed in the open, off to the side. It was visible through a round hole in the center where a part of the ceiling had fallen in. No one knew what the purpose of this underground chamber had been. In my fantasies it had once been a meeting place of a secret roundtable similar to the one King Arthur and his knights had attended. Nearby was a ruined swimming pool. The whole rise was covered with stately beech and oak trees and a jumble of shrubbery interspersed with patches of grass. There were lots of rabbits in this coppice and in the park. When I was still at home, I had shot a few with my .22 caliber rifle for the kitchen.

The house, looking like a small French chateau, had been built around 1875 by one of the top managers of the Heye glass works. He had also established the park and filled it with rare imported trees and exotic bushes that yielded a profusion of fragrant- smelling blossoms in summer. A tennis court behind our garden had been turned into a vegetable garden by the people who lived on the first floor under us. Behind it, at the foot of the rise, was an artificial pond large enough for rowboats, and a grotto with a balustrade over it where musicians once entertained guests.

There must have been great parties during the heyday of the estate until the creator-owner went bankrupt, took a pistol into the park and shot himself. It was rumored that he had meddled in alchemy. After his death the house fell into disrepair and the park into neglect. The estate became the property of the glass factory. A single woman lived for many years in the house and died there. Thereafter, the two floors were rented out to two families whose husbands held positions in the factory. That was how we came to live there. The park and the thickets around the tower, called "*die Ruine*" throughout Gerresheim, became my personal hunting ground where I roamed unobserved when I was home.

We picked some ripe gooseberries and sat on a bench. My parents wanted to know about my time in Bad Einsiedel. I tried to tell them but I still felt awkward. When it was dark we went back into the house. My parents had to get up at 5:30 A.M. because my father had to be in the factory well before 7 A.M., when work started. His office and the machine shop were about one kilometer from our house. He walked. He had developed difficulties breathing, my mother told me, and he had to take his time.

Before my parents went to bed, my mother put a little black-leather suitcase next to the door. She always took it with her into the cellar when sirens sounded the alarm. The suitcase held what little jewelry she owned and our family's most important papers and documents.

I said good night and took a bath. Afterward, in my own soft bed, so different from the Spartan cot in Einsiedel, I looked at my room as if I had never seen it before: the bookshelves, table and chair, the twelve volumes of the Brockhaus Encyclopedia, the two crossed dueling swords I would never have a use for, my rifle on the wall, the Plaster of Paris copy of the death mask of the philosopher F. W. Nietzsche above my bed, one of the writers I admired. The sweet song of a nightingale came through the dark. I listened and eventually I fell asleep. There was no alarm that night.

After breakfast I talked for a while with my mother. Then I took the rifle and went down to the park, working my way slowly toward the rise and up to the tower. I sat down on a stone that had fallen from the crest. I saw songbirds and wild pigeons, but no rabbits.

I was not really looking for them. I had only taken the rifle as something familiar, something to hold on to, something to suggest a direction, a purpose, although I had none. I was thinking about other things than game. This was my last day at home. I wondered what would happen to us, to me. After my time as *Flakhelfer* I would wind up in the *Heer*. My school days, in terms of an earlier sense of what school should be were over. Until the end of the war, whenever that might be, I would only return to this place on furlough, or not at all. I looked over the wild green jumble around me. How beautiful it was.

2

Flakhelfer, Reisholz
June 10 1943-January 18 1944

Arrival. June 10 1943. On a sunny morning, Ferdi and I took the no. 3 tram from Gerresheim at 7 A.M., switched to no. 18 downtown and arrived at 8:30 at the stop in Reisholz, a suburb on the southern edge of the city. We had just passed the spread of buildings of the Henkel Chemical Factory. The tram left, continuing toward Benrath, a small town grouped around a Rococo castle and a vast park. We were the only persons who got off. Directly west, across the road, a short distance away but hidden by a tree line lay the wide river bed through which the Rhine churned north. To the east was a large open rye field. From the standing waves of grain in the southeastern corner of the field rose twelve grass-covered revetments closely grouped in two clusters. From each of the revetments protruded the long, dark-grey barrel of an 8.8cm gun, all pointing in the same direction. Later we learned that the initial position of the barrels was 45 degrees in direction 10 o'clock (WNW). Before us was the *4. Schwere Flakabteilung 177/0.*

Ferdi and I stood for a long moment and gazed at the image before us. I looked with awe and apprehension. We had seen batteries like this one in many of the half-hour newsreels that were shown in movie theaters before the motion picture. They were usually filmed in action, with streaks of flames leaping from the guns' muzzles into the night sky. But here, I was no longer a movie-goer seated in the comfort of a darkened theater. Before me lay my assigned place, my future. I was to become part of this. The guns lay silent at the moment but represented a constant threat. I felt small and vulnerable. I wanted nothing more than to turn back, away from this. I couldn't. We gripped our small suitcases with essential books, writing materials, a few personal items – and trudged on to deliver ourselves. We did not speak.

We took the dirt road to the battery and skirted the southern edge of the rye field. After half a kilometer we reached the underground bunkers of the *Mess-Staffel*, the fire-control post, with two radar stations on top and two revetments that enclosed fire-control predictors of the battery. The road curved past the wooden barracks of the *Mess-Staffel* personnel and the first of the gun emplacements and continued. Nearby stood two barracks closed in with a high wire fence. It was the camp of the *Hiwis, Hilfswillige* – Russian prisoners of war who had volunteered service as auxiliaries in the German anti-aircraft arm. Behind this camp a line of wooden barracks extended north along railroad tracks – the quarters of the *Geschütz-Staffel*, the gun crews. We crossed the railroad tracks that ran north to the factory from two depots below the southern perimeter of the battery and met a *Flakhelfer* dressed in *Luftwaffe* fatigues.

He told us that he was from Hilden *Gymnasium* and had been with the first batch of students called up in February. He eyed us, bemused and a little condescending. He had the air of an *alter Hase* ('old hare'), one who had been under fire and proven himself. To him, Ferdi and I were untested latecomers. He pointed to a group of trucks visible on the hardtop street ahead, at the edge of a birch forest. Barely protruding over treetops was the large circular shape of a searchlight, designed to illuminate enemy aircraft on clear nights. Covered with a tarp it was positioned on a wooden tower. Near the trucks we found the *Tross-Staffel*, a group of barracks set into the birch forest. They included the headquarters of the *Abteilung*, mess hall, kitchen, weapons' and supplies' depots, first aid and sick bay, and the barracks of the *Tross-Staffel* personnel. At the first barrack, we showed our induction papers to a Corporal. He sent us to headquarters.

Through the open door we heard the clicking sound of typewriters and saw two *Flakhelferinnen* hunched over their machines. A heavy-set man in the uniform of a sergeant-major viewed us suspiciously and waved us in. He rose from the chair behind his desk. In German *Landser* jargon the sergeant-major, any sergeant-major or *Spiess*, was cynically called "mother of the company," suggesting usually the opposite, something like "son-of-a-bitch." This man turned out to be no exception. He was brusque and gruff. We showed him our papers. He grunted and seemed to memorize our names. He did not ask us anything. He said curtly, "Nine others of your group came yesterday. I sent four to the *Mess-Staffel.* Six go to the *Geschütz-Staffel.*" He looked at Ferdi. "You are assigned to Corporal Waldmüller, gun Anton. You," he turned to me, "go to Corporal Tylia, gun Bertha." He signaled to a lance-corporal to take us outside. We noticed that the secretaries, girls in their mid-twenties, were dressed in white blouses and skirts in blue *Luftwaffe* colors. The sergeant-major, in a heavy South German accent, called after us, "Report to your gun chiefs. Come back tomorrow for your *Luftwaffenhelfer-Ausweis* (identification card)."

At the quartermaster's we tried on dark grey fatigues until we found some that matched our sizes. The dress uniform was the standard uniform of the "*Flieger HJ*" branch of the Hitler Youth: tunic, ski pants and ski cap in light blue with the removable swastika armband to wear on the upper left arm. A small black triangle in cloth over the right breast pocket with a blue *Luftwaffe* eagle in the center and the letters L H in capital on top identified the wearer as a *Luftwaffenhelfer*. Having never been members of the Hitler Youth proper, Ferdi and I accepted the dress uniform as a step backward, but inevitable. We also got the balance of our new dress: blue shirts and a tie, underwear, shoes and socks, towels, toiletries, heavy overcoats, gas masks, cumbersome steel helmets that did not fit our heads well, and cotton balls to plug our ears during shooting. We piled our gear on a little four-wheel cart and, with the lance-corporal leading, set off for our cabin by the depot.

It was a shack, about seven by five meters, with a flat roof, a wooden door, and two windows on one side. Behind the door were six lockers, two small tables, three bunk beds with two cots each. Two upper cots were not yet taken. It seemed they were for us. There was no running water except for an outside faucet. The outdoor toilet, we were told, was a one-seater on the west side of the depot, about 250 meters away. Before the soldier left with the cart, we asked directions to guns Anton and Bertha. We changed into fatigues, stowed our gear in two empty lockers, and went toward the gun revetments. We crossed the railroad tracks and, behind the Russian camp, asked an elderly soldier where we could find the gun chiefs we had been ordered to see. He pointed to a line of barracks and singled out two.

Through the open door I got my first look at Corporal Tylia. I hesitated and stopped. He sat with his back to me but had heard my footsteps. He got up and turned around. Slender, medium-sized, he looked at me with a question in his eyes. I said haltingly, something like, I had to report to him because the sergeant-major had assigned me to him and his gun. He asked for my name and where I lived, where I had been. After I told him, he said, "I'll call you Paulchen." I don't know why and he never told me. Perhaps he knew a Paulchen and I looked similar to the one he knew. Or I simply looked, for other reasons, like a Paulchen to him. He always called me by that name during the many months I was stationed in Reisholz with him. He always acted somewhat fatherly toward me. There must have been something special for him about that name. Corporal Tylia was a friendly, at times melancholic, homesick man from East Prussia. He cared little about military etiquette but was strict in everything involving the gun, demanding flawless performance from the crew when in action.

After he had given me a name, he told me that the gun crews were all unloading an ammunition train that had arrived earlier. He told me to come with him. He wanted to show me my workplace. The six gun emplacements of 2nd Battery were next to those of 1st Battery. They were arranged in circles with one in the center. The distance from gun to gun was about 60 meters. Bertha was in the northeast location of 2nd Battery. The grass-covered revetment was circular, higher than a tall person and a couple of meters thick. The entrance was at an angle and switched direction inside the wall so that the interior was not exposed should a bomb explode in front of it. The big gun was mounted on the four extensions of the gun carriage affixed to the ground (*Kreuzlafette*). On the inside, vertical timber planks held the wall. On one side was a bunker, shelter for the crew in bad weather when no immediate action was expected. A number of wooden doors covered the other sides. The space behind contained stacked ammunition crates with three shells apiece. Together they comprised 180 rounds, the Corporal told me. This number appeared sufficient for a night's shooting. Occasionally up to 150 rounds, or *Gruppen*, had been fired during an especially turbulent night.

He took me to the gun and explained the various positions. On the left side of the gun stood the K 1 (*Kanonier* 1, gunner 1), the elevation gun-layer, next to him, the K 2 (*Kanonier* 2, gunner 2), the azimuth gun-layer. The fuse setter, the K 6, sat on the right side on a seat in front of the fuse setting machine. These three positions were filled with *Flakhelfer*. They were boys from my school, he informed me. The ammunition gunners, K 4, K 5 and K 7 were Russians. The tasks of K 5 and K 7 were to supply the K 4 with shells that he would slip with their tips into the two receiving cups of the fuse setting machine. The K 3, the loader, was a lance-corporal. Tylia himself, the gun chief, would stand a few steps behind the gun during firing. I would be required to serve in the K 1, K2 and K 6 positions, rotating from one to the other. It would prevent boredom and keep us sharp.

I don't remember how I took the introduction to Bertha. I am sure the chief meant well and wanted to familiarize me a little with the gun before I, a complete novice, was added to a crew that operated as a well-functioning organism. He might have known that Paulchen was overwhelmed. He smiled briefly when he was through. He walked with me to where the crews of both batteries worked at the ammo bunkers unloading an ammunition train. He introduced me to the three *Flakhelfer* of his team. I knew them from my school. They had not been in the KLV program and thus were drafted to Reisholz in February. They knew the ropes. There was a bit of distance between us because they were not of the Einsiedel bunch. Circumstance and a few days would change that.

I worked alongside them, lugging crates that weighed about a hundred pounds and carrying crates with empties that weighed much less. Much of the heavy lifting was done by the Russians. I saw Ferdi and the other four who had been in Einsiedel: Thei, Hannes, Bergittimus and Wenner, room mates in the shack by the depot, our new home. They were already blending in.

Before noon the train had been unloaded and took off with a cargo of crates with empty shell cases. Soldiers and *Flakhelfer* walked to lunch at the mess hall in the birch forest, a mere 350 meters away. *Flakhelfer* of 2nd Battery and some working in the *Mess-Staffel* were from Rethel *Gymnasium*. Those with 1st Battery, including a few in the *Mess-Staffel*, were from Hilden *Gymnasium*. The Rethel kids sat with their NCOs and soldiers while the Hilden kids ate with their teammates. There was not much exchange between the two groups of *Flakhelfer* even though they were members of one *Grosskampfbatterie* (term for a battery that combined two enlarged regular batteries for added firepower) and shared identical tasks. Perhaps a sort of buddy system was used here. The boys who had grown up and been in school together were allowed to stay together. There was no competition between the two groups. Performance levels were the same.

Where soldiers and *Flakhelfer* strolled in small groups to the mess hall everyday, the Russians made a dramatic entry. They gathered at their camp, formed in ranks and marched up in military fashion, singing Russian marching songs. They were led by their commander, a German Sergeant, who spoke Russian fluently and lived and slept in one of their barracks. He mostly stayed away from other German soldiers and his fellow NCOs. From the Russians he demanded an excessive discipline and punished any transgression severely.

Lunch was the only time the members of the batteries came together. Breakfast at 0800 (0900 after a night alarm) and supper, at 1800, were collected by individual barracks at the kitchen. Often, for supper, big jugs of a sweet milk and noodle soup were added specifically for *Flakhelfer* to the regular fare of cold food and coffee. We did not like this creation much. What we could not finish, and that was most of it, we passed on to the Russians who had greater appetite than us kids and seemed to be genuinely fond of the sweet stuff.

After lunch, on that first afternoon in Reisholz, Corporal Tylia told Werner and Walter, two of the *Flakhelfer* of the Bertha crew, to show me, after the midday break, what kind of work they did on the gun. I met them at 1400 in the revetment. Gun-layer K 1 (elevation), K 2 (azimuth) and K 6 (fuse setting) operated their controls with wheels like the steering wheel of a car, following a command pointer with the position pointer. During fire alarm the shifting command pointers on the screens of the three positions had to be covered precisely and fully with the position pointers regardless of what happened within the embankment, outside or in the sky above. At first glance that did not seem difficult. But considering the ear-splitting noise of firing, the bucking of the gun, rapid changes of direction and elevation, stumbling over the extension of the gun carriage and empty shell cases thrown over the ground, it was hard to stay glued to the pointers in front of one's eyes.

This they told me. Because we were not in alarm phase, the system was not on and they could not demonstrate how it was done. That could only happen during action – perhaps that night or the next night, they thought. They shrugged. They said that the battery had been in action at least twice a week and on an air raid alert almost every other night. They said that the English attacked during the night, the Americans during the day. The Americans had begun bombing in early February 1943, mostly cities along the North Sea coast. Only twice, so far, they had attacked a city close to the Ruhr, Hamm. The boys had not seen American planes yet. The English came almost every night, bombing cities somewhere in Germany. Sometimes, on their way back, the stream of bombers came close enough that the Reisholz 8.8 could reach them.

Werner pulled a calendar notebook from his breast pocket. He flipped through the pages. "From May 1 to today, June 10, let's see, the English bombed close to us…" he counted slowly, "eight times: Essen, May 1, Dortmund May 5, Duisburg, May 13, Bochum, May 14, Dortmund again, May 24, Düsseldorf, yes, our city, May 26, Essen again, May 28, Wuppertal, May 30." He paused. "During some of these raids we did a lot of shooting, especially during the attack on our city and on Wuppertal." He put his notebook away. They looked at each other.

"We saw many cities burn," Walter said. "Sometimes you can see the fires from a hundred kilometers away or more. Clouds turn red in the sky from the fires below. Smoke hangs in the air for days afterward." He stopped. He had talked about something they had already seen too often.

"How are your parents?" I asked.

"We were lucky, they were lucky. The Altstadt was partly destroyed," Werner said. He sighed. " The parts where our parents live did not get hit much."

We were silent for a while. Then I asked about school in the battery. They laughed. "We are supposed to have school Monday to Wednesday in the mess hall after lunch. But sometimes we don't. We either have a readiness call or the teacher could not make it because the city was under air raid alarm and all traffic had stopped."

"Who are the teachers?" I asked.

"Pedi and Wallerich." Pedi was the nickname for Dr. Peltzer who taught Latin and History. He was a friendly man, popular among students and generous with grades. Wallerich I knew from the Bad Spindelmühle KLV camp. He was a fine math teacher, demanding but patient, understanding.

They asked me about Bad Einsiedel and I told them. They listened with little interest. What I described seemed to them far away, a fairyland. I was beginning to feel that way too. Einsiedel was quickly becoming a blur, retreating before a new and harsh reality.

They told me something I was eager to hear. *Flakhelfer* were allowed two weekend furloughs a month to visit with their parents, provided their positions in the battery were covered by someone else. Because we six newcomers had been added as fourth *Flakhelfer* per gun, a few of the old crews had a chance to get a furlough on the next weekend. By then we were expected to be fit for action. I saw Einsiedel slipping away even further into the shadows.

We talked a little more about things that concerned us. Shortly before 1800, the time for supper, I left to join my old buddies in the shack by the railroad depot. Our reunion was subdued. Too much had happened that day. Two of us went for our food but we ate as if chewing wood. The coffee can – coffee not made from real coffee beans but from a substitute, a sorry tasting brew – was cleaned and returned to the kitchen. We talked briefly about the people we had met. We went to our cots early. There was no alarm during the night.

Whit Saturday, June 11-12. At 0700 the bell on the wall in our shack rang out the wake- up call. The same bell would chase us out of bed for a night alarm. I .had made the acquaintance of the outhouse the night before. I paid it another visit in the morning and, in daylight, admired the decorations on the walls. They were from German magazines, photographs from musicals highlighting scores of scantily dressed dance girls. After washing up and putting our shack in order, Ferdi, Thei and I went for our breakfast. It consisted of *Kommissbrot*, the typical fare of rye bread baked for the military, a sliver of margarine, a hard slice of a honey substitute, a small cut of sausage and the obligatory coffee. When we had eaten we went to our gun emplacements.

I was introduced to the K 3, the loader, a muscular, quiet lance-corporal. The gun chief explained the mechanism of the 8.8cm gun to me and showed me every feature within the revetment. He gave me a brochure to study. It contained pictures of enemy aircraft and information about the capabilities of each. The types that naturally most concerned the Flak gunners in Germany were *Viermots*, four-engined bombers. English *Viermots* were the Stirling, Halifax and Lancaster. Of these the Lancaster was regarded as the best plane. American *Viermots* were the B 17 Fortress and the B 24 Liberator. Both were rumored to be as good as the Lancaster although they had not yet to be seen in our neighborhood. The one type that was an enigma was the Mosquito, a two-engine English plane of great speed that served as pathfinder and marked the target area for the bomber stream. Rarely was one shot down. The plane's body was largely built of wood to escape radar detection. On cloudless nights a pathfinder was sometimes caught by searchlights and rode the apex of light beams from the ground prior to an attack. The attack was preceded by light cascades in red and green dropped by the Mosquito. We called these *Christbäume* ("Christmas trees").

After lunch we spent the midday break in our shack talking. We had learned the essentials. Our home base was the shack where we slept and ate our breakfast and supper. We knew where headquarters and the mess hall were. We knew the gun and crew we had been attached to, the ammo bunkers, both those beside the railroad tracks and the ones in the gun revetments. The first were the sources from which those at the gun were replenished after a shoot. And we knew our outhouse. Our life from then on would revolve around these points. Our world was as narrow as it had been in Einsiedel but more regulated, less open, a lot simpler if not entirely primitive. We had been thrown into something that we did not yet understand. We couldn't articulate this well, but we felt it. We were somehow reassured because the kids who had come here in February must have felt the same way at the beginning. They had gotten through it. They seemed to be all right.

After the break we went to headquarters where our photos were taken and we received our *Flakhelfer* identification cards. We were informed that *Flakhelfer* received a pay of 0,50 *Reichsmark* (50 pennies) per day and that travel by means of public transformation was free to us. The afternoon we spent again with our respective guns and crews. In the Bertha revetment, that included the three Russian ammunition gunners who served as K 4, K 5, and K 7. They wore fragments of Russian uniforms supplemented with *Luftwaffe* fatigues. Two were in their late twenties, one in his early thirties. These were the first Russians I had seen in person and I tried not to gawk at them. At first glance they seemed guarded. Many turned out to be pretty good men, with whom we spent the long nights standing together by the revetment wall staring into the dark. We tried to communicate with each other across the chasm created by the war. Neither I nor they, nor anyone else, was in control of anything, least of all concerning our personal fates. They learned a little more German from us. I learned, in exchange, a little Russian including a remarkable set of Russian swearwords. As members of the gun crew they proved to be dependable under any circumstances.

After supper was leisure time. We spent it reading and having small talk. At 2100 the light had to be out and we went to our cots.

The bell rang after 2300. Alarm! We jumped onto the wooden floor and quickly dressed. We grabbed overcoats, steel helmets and gas masks and rushed out. There was a solid cloud cover and the ground lay in darkness. We went as quickly as was possible. Because our shack was farthest from the guns, I arrived at Bertha last.

The crew stood in a group around the gun. My eyes got used to the dark and I could distinguish faces. The chief wore headphones and a microphone. He listened to the command post. He and the K 3 were smoking cigarettes. The three Russians smoked hand-rolled cigarettes of the rough, grainy Russian *machorka* tobacco they got in their rations. *Flakhelfer* were not allowed to smoke. Faces were somber, those of the kids too. They had been through this before. No one spoke. We stood in silence for quite a while. We waited. The land all around us, including the city just to the north lay in complete darkness.

The chief raised his hand. Information was being passed to him from the command post. "Bomber formations approaching the Dutch coast, nearing Amsterdam," he said. This did not have to mean much to us. Amsterdam was about 180 kilometers northwest of Düsseldorf. If the bombers stayed on their present course they would bypass us by about 125 kilometers, going for a target farther east.

We waited.

After about twenty minutes the next report came in. "Leading formations over Arnhem." The bombers had changed directions. Arnhem was less than 100 kilometers WNW. Throughout the Ruhr area, from Bottrop to Essen and Duisburg, the air raid alarm for the civilian populations would be given. Some time passed, then, far away to the north, we saw the bottom of the dense mass of clouds lit by the brilliant white-blue tentacles of searchlights, moving around, fingers of doom touching but not penetrating the mass above. The Flak crews and nightfighter pilots called this ghostly spectacle *Leichentuch*, "the shroud." Because of impaired

Map of the Northern Rhineland and the Ruhr District.

visibility, optical instruments were of no help and the batteries would be directed by radar.

Waiting. Finally, "Get ready, the chief said. We put our helmets on. I was nudged by someone and reminded to plug my ears with cotton balls. The crew took up positions. The Russians opened the ammo bunkers. The K 6 mounted the chair in front of the fuse setting machine. "Gun position 11," the chief shouted. The K 2 wheeled the gun in this direction.

It did not take long and the report came, "Leading formations over Goch." Now they were 60 kilometers away. There still was no telling what their target would be. Perhaps another attack on one of the Ruhr cities, Essen, Duisburg, or some other? The chief reported to the command post, "Gun Bertha ready."

Some time later the searchlights around Düsseldorf picked up from those of Duisburg, a ring of lights reaching from the ground to the clouds. Fifteen more minutes. In the dark city before us the air raid sirens screamed and howled. Corporal Tylia called to me "Stand under the barrel if we get to fire."

More time passed and the command pointers of the K 1, K 2 and K 6 positions lit up. The Russians formed a line, cradling shells in their arms. The K 4 embedded two in the cups of the fuse setting machine. "*Abgedeckt*," covered, shouted K 1, K2 and K 6.

The K 3, a heavy leather glove on his right arm, stood next to the fuse setter, ready to pull a shell out and lift it into the breechblock of the cannon. "Covered," the gun chief said into the microphone. "Direction 12," he called to the K 2.

Suddenly, around the northern part of the city, heavy Flak opened up, first 12.8cm and 10.5cm guns, then 8.8. Now, over the anti-aircraft fire, we heard the dull rumble of the approaching bomber fleet. All of a sudden, cascades of red light appeared in the *Leichentuch* above the city, descending very slowly. "*Gruppenfeuer*," the chief shouted. "*Gruppe*!"

I hurried obediently to a position under the barrel. The explosion hit me like a tumbling wall. I thought my eardrums had burst. I staggered and moved quickly away. "*Gruppe*" followed "*Gruppe*." Over the crashing of the gun I heard another sound, the terrible roar of many explosions that seemed to make the earth shake. These added to the explosions in the air over the city from many heavy anti-aircraft guns to make a constant deafening thunder. I stood helplessly pressed against the embankment, the helmet slipped over my eyes. I shoved it back and, frightened as never before, stared shaken at the action before me. The K 3 lifted the heavy shells out of the fuse setting cups, thrust them in to the breechblock and pulled the fire lever. Empty shell cases littered the ground. With each round another was thrown from the breech and landed with a clanking sound. The gun fired and bucked but the crew seemed oblivious of what was going on elsewhere.

The bombing continued and, slowly at first, then broadening, cones of fire emerged from the city, growing into a wide field of flames that threw a red cast into the clouds. I saw black smoke and saw *Christbäume* in green replace the red ones as the bombing went on. The gun chief called to me and pointed to the K 1. "Stand behind him, watch!" he shouted over the din. I did, eager not to be a useless observer. I stood behind Walter who manipulated the wheel in covering the command pointer. I tried to focus on his chore so I would not hear the continuing explosions from the city and might ignore the roar of the bombers flying over us after they had dropped their loads. Sometimes I glanced into the sky where the fire of our battery, and that of other batteries around the city, was concentrated. I couldn't see much because of the thick clouds that had turned red from the burning city.

And then it was over. The bombers were gone but a large part of the city was aflame. The fires continued to spread. Columns of black smoke rose into the sky. We stood by the parapet and looked toward the city in silence. The adults smoked cigarettes, the boys stood without. I suppose I was in shock. Our parents were on our minds. The Reisholz *4. Schwere Flakabteilung 177/0* alone fired 156 *Gruppen*. Other batteries had done their best, too, but we had not prevented the destruction before our eyes. The air raid had taken perhaps forty-five minutes. We stood and watched. There was nothing we could do. Before we dispersed the gun chief called me over. "Sorry, Paulchen," he said. "I had to do this." Although it had been a cruel joke, I learned that it was considered a baptism of fire to put a novice under the barrel. Now I had become a member of the crew, sort of.

I plodded to our shack, my path lit by the burning city. Two of my buddies were already there, the others came one by one. We did not say much. We had shared the same experience. The homes of five of us, Ferdi, Thei, Bergittimus, Wenner and I were in Gerresheim. Because the raid seemed to have concentrated on the center of the city we convinced ourselves that our families were safe. But Hannes' parents lived in Flingern, a suburb about two kilometers east of the main Düsseldorf railroad station. How were they? Hannes stared glumly at the floor between his feet. We tried a few words to cheer him. There were more *Flakhelfer* in Hannes' shoes. For the soldiers and Russian *Hiwis* it was different. They were not from this city. Home was at some other place. They would not suffer a personal tragedy here, although they would worry about what could happen to their own homes somewhere else. A lot of quiet worrying went on.

None of the *Flakhelfer* was given even a brief leave to check on their families. We were regarded as indispensable for the operation of the battery. Direct phone connections with the *Flakhelfer* homes did not exist. Very few civilian households were allowed a phone. Because communication systems in the city had been greatly disrupted, it took two days for parents to find ways to call the battery from somewhere outside and let their sons know how they were. My father phoned the battery from the factory. Headquarters informed me that Gerresheim had been spared.

The first three weeks, June 12-July 2. The bell rang wake-up at 0800. We dressed and did our morning chores in the shack before Bergittimus and I visited the kitchen for our breakfast rations. Smoke flags to the north indicated that parts of the city were still burning. After breakfast we went to the gun revetments. All of the *Geschütz-Staffel* personnel worked through the morning and part of the afternoon. Empty shell cases were gathered and stacked at the railroad track and, from supply bunkers there, the ammo bunkers in the gun revetments were refilled. We would need another ammo train soon. Later in the afternoon the gun barrel was cleaned. Routine tasks left little time to ponder the events of the past hours.

But after work, we finally had time to think. Watching the smoke drifting east with a western wind, I imagined pictures I had seen before: rubble-filled streets, fire- blackened façades of collapsed houses with empty window holes, wrecked vehicles and streetcars, twisted steel tracks, people tearing at wreckage to get to those buried underneath. People sitting dazed, the elderly, women and children, with what little they saved, others moving away from the ruins while firefighters, Red Cross and emergency teams were still moving in. And still fires burned, burning themselves out slowly. Bodies carried away by rescue squads. First aid posts. Wuppertal-Barmen had been a reminder to us after months of seclusion in Bad Einsiedel, but the wounds of that city were nine days old when we passed through. Our city was hit only hours ago; the wounds were fresh.

Slowly the horror of it seeped into our minds. We spoke little that evening. Each of us lived in his own thoughts. We went to bed early. We were tired, physically and emotionally.

The alarm bell woke us after 0100.

We jumped from our bunks, dressed quickly and ran from the shack. The night sky was not as dark as on the night before. Thin clouds drifted by slowly, leaving openings through which one could see a clear sky, even a glimmer of stars. This time I arrived before the Russians. Around the gun the situation was the same as on the previous night. The adults smoked cigarettes and we *Flakhelfer* stood quietly without smoking. Corporal Tylia wore headphones and microphone but no report was coming in yet. The fires from the city had diminished but we still could smell smoke.

We waited. When the first report came it sounded like a repetition of the night before. "Bomber formations approaching the Dutch coast," the gun chief said. "This time they are farther south, direction Rotterdam. "

Rotterdam was 140 kilometers northwest of Düsseldorf. What we had learned in geography in school proved worthwhile. As last night, there was no telling what direction the English would take after passing over Rotterdam. I wondered aloud if they would come for us again. "Probably not," Walter said. "They usually don't attack the same city twice in two nights." He paused. "It has happened, though."

I was not convinced. Fear gripped me again as it had last night. I tried to shake it off but could not.

Time passed and the next report, repeated by the gun chief to us, said, "Leading formations approaching Nijmegen." The bombers were closing in on the German border but still continuing east. They were, however, 50 kilometers away from the western edge of the Ruhr, the heart of the German industrial complex. Again, as last night, the air raid alarm would be given from Gelsenkirchen to Bottrop, Recklinghaunsen, Oberhausen, Mülheim, Duisburg, Essen, Bochum, Dortmund. If they attacked somewhere in the Ruhr, any of these cities could be a target. Each of them had been attacked dozens of times before.

And then, to the north, we saw the ghostly fingers of hundreds of searchlights reach into the sky.

The next report said, "Leading formations over Emmerich, turning south." Tylia shouted, "Get ready!" We put on helmets. The Russians opened the ammo bunkers and stood by. The crew took up positions. "Direction 12," the gun chief called. "Paulchen! Stand behind K 1!"

"They are using the Rhine to guide them," someone said. Seen from the bombers, the river was probably a silvery band below, easy to follow. Where would they go? I felt the tension of the crew. Minutes ticked away.

"Southeast of Wesel, lading formations have turned southeast," repeated Tylia the information passed on by the command post.

A sigh of relief. It would be one of the Ruhr cities again. Which one? Suddenly the sirens of Düsseldorf filled the air with their screams, sending the population into the air raid shelters. It seemed *Luftschutz* officials would take no chances. But searchlights around the city were not yet on.

Waiting. Time passed slowly. "*Christbäume*," the gun chief said. "Northeast." Information came in from the command post. "Heavy air raid on Bochum," Tylia repeated. We left our positions for a moment and looked over the revetment wall. Despite the distance, red lights could be clearly be seen, hanging low in the sky and drifting down ever so slowly. Bochum was about 40 kilometers northeast of Düsseldorf. We heard the faint rumble of massed explosions and, where we thought Bochum was, the sky lit up as it might during a violent thunderstorm.

"Back to the gun," the Corporal snarled. When we got back to our positions, he said, "They might come our way as they go back. Get ready. "

He was right. It did not take long for the command post to relay that the first enemy formations had turned southwest after the bomb run and would pass to the north of us. At that moment the searchlights around Düsseldorf flooded the sky, lighting slim clouds and revealing vast spaces beyond. The command pointers appeared on the illuminated dials in front of the K 1, K 2 and K 6. Shells were lifted into the cups of the fuse setting machine. The three gunners shouted, "*Abgedeckt*!" and the chief called "Covered!" into the mic "Direction 2." The gun whirled to the new direction.

We heard the faint sound of approaching air planes, growing louder, swelling into a steady growl. Looking up, I saw that the searchlights had found three *Viermots*, it seemed Lancasters. Although they twisted and rolled to escape the blinding light, the glowing tentacles stayed with them. Heavy guns north of Düsseldorf opened up and surrounded the planes with bursting shells. One was hit and fell, flaming wreckage, to the ground.

The bombers were too far away for our battery to join the action. New *Pulks* of planes were picked up by the searchlights and were exposed to massive Flak fire. With short intervals this went on for nearly 30 minutes. At last the Corporal called, "Direction 3! Report!" "*Abgedeckt*!" the gunners shouted. It seemed that stragglers from the bomber stream had come into our range. "*Gruppenfeuer*! *Gruppe*!" The gun crashed and bucked. I held on to Walter, following his work closely. After six *Gruppen*, Tylia called, "Paulchen, take the K 1." Walter stepped aside and I grabbed the wheel. He looked over my shoulder. It did not seem hard to follow the command pointer with the position pointer, but it was – not physically so much but mentally. I had to focus my mind and my hands completely on overlaying one pointer with the other, and keeping them together regardless if one tried to budge from the other. I tried desperately to do it right, although I was aware that I slipped briefly a few times.

While Bochum was burning, lighting the horizon to the clouds, we fired a total of 31 *Gruppen* that night, and I served as K 1 on 25. Walter was reassuring when it was over. Tylia measured me gravely, then his face relaxed. I think he thought Paulchen had done all right.

This was the night of June 12-13. I took a clue from Werner and kept a diary that included air raids on the Ruhr and Rhineland, and our activities during the raids. I started the diary with the Whit Saturday raid on Düsseldorf, June 11-12. What happened to other cities and targets elsewhere in Germany was not my immediate concern.

At around 0300 the gun crews were released. In the shack we were too tired to talk and took to the cots immediately. When the wake-up call came at 0800 we were barely able to get up. We dressed and did the usual chores around our place like sleepwalkers. We munched breakfast listlessly. When I went to the Bertha gun later I found the Russians cleaning the revetment, removing shell cases and refilling the ammo bunkers. Beside cleaning the gun barrel there was not much to do. Corporal Tylia was reasonable enough not to submit us to senseless labor just to kill time. But I learned quickly that one of the major snags in the life of a *Flakhelfer*, or an adult soldier, was boredom.

Of the soldiers, some sought diversion through sexual escapades with local girls or lonely women during late hours in the nearby birch forest. We *Flakhelfer* were too young, too innocent and inexperienced to attempt to join in. There was a recognizable undercurrent of sexuality in the batteries. It was the result of healthy Flak soldiers placed amidst a civilian population traumatized by constant danger, with husbands and sons away on military service in distant places. The Russians were involved too. The Sergeant in charge of their camp let some slip out at night to meet Ukrainian women from a nearby camp of forced laborers who toiled in the Henkel factory during daytime.

The six of us, when we were together, talked little about our new experiences. Each of us dealt with them individually. I turned to books I had brought with me. I had known for many years that reading good books could help me escape from where I was and slip into a world opened by the passages and pages before me.

The day passed. There was no night alarm.

But a day later the alarm bell threw us out of bed at 2350. What came turned out to be nearly identical to the events of two nights earlier. Again the English bomber stream flew in over the Dutch coast, sought the Rhine and followed it southeast on another night with broken clouds. We stood by the gun and waited. Most of our time during an air raid alarm was spent waiting. When action came, it usually came quickly and violently.

This time the target was Oberhausen, a city next to Essen, both cities, along with Bochum and Gelsenkirchen, the heart of the Kohlenpott, the Ruhr industrial center. Oberhausen was a mere 30 kilometers away and almost straight north of us. Sirens in Düsseldorf gave the general alarm. Toward the north, over a wide area, we saw massed searchlights reach into the sky. The distant rumble of heavy Flak fire. And again, low over the horizon, we saw red *Christbäume* dropped by Mosquitoes, Christmas trees of death. The sound of the Flak fire mixed with the dull sounds of explosions on the ground. We stood and watched. Blood-red mushrooms of fires sprang up from the earth. They grew and expanded and colored the bottoms of clouds passing overhead.

We were told to man our positions. I was again to be the K 1. On their way out the bombers might come into our range. The searchlights around Düsseldorf got into action, penetrating the thin cast of drifting clouds, reaching far into the sky. Batteries well north of our city opened up. Once again I saw airplanes caught by white beams, riding the cones of concentrated lights, encircled by puffs of exploding shells. While this went on we stood idle. Most of the *Viermots* turned west to the north of us. Finally one formation came close enough. All the batteries around the city leapt into action. Our battery fired eighteen *Gruppen*. Then the *Pulk* had passed. No visible kill of a *Viermot* over or near Düsseldorf was reported. It seemed to me that these planes were close to invulnerable. We could not stop them. Once more I had served as K 1. I was beginning to get used to it. This was the night of June 14-15.

On Whitsun Monday, June 13, a legal holiday, no newspaper was published in the city. But on the following day we learned from the newspaper that the night raid on Whit Saturday had largely destroyed the central part of Düsseldorf, plowing a ragged swath roughly two and a half kilometers long and one and a half kilometers wide. The area of impact extended from Derendorf in the north to the main railroad station in the south. The raid had taken the lives of 1,298 identified civilians, left thousands missing or injured, and 140,000 people homeless. The bomb carpet dropped by the *Viermots* had ended about three kilometers north of our battery.

This is from my diary. I did not chronicle the casualty numbers of the Bochum and Oberhausen raids.

On Tuesday, June 14 and on Wednesday, June 15, we should have had school in the battery but it was canceled. Due to the devastation, traffic in much of the city had been paralyzed. Neither of our two teachers, if they were alive, had a chance to get to us. It turned out that school was resumed only on Monday, July 5.

Over the following two weeks of June, within a radius of 50 kilometers, we saw more cities burn around us: Köln the night of 16-17, Krefeld on the night of 21-22, Mülheim on the night of 22-23, Wuppertal, again, on the night of 24-25, Gelsenkirchen and Solingen on the night of 25-26, and Köln, again, on the night of 28-29. This last raid was most severe. I recorded the information as: 4,377 identified civilians dead, thousands missing or injured, 250,000 homes lost to bombs and a firestorm.

Düsseldorf was attacked again during this period, on the night of 25-26, the same night as Gelsenkirchen and Solingen. This time the Old Town area was hit once more, crumbling more parts of this ancient, beautiful quarter by the Rhine.

During these attacks I alternately served in all three *Flakhelfer* positions, K 1, K 2, and K 6. During the Düsseldorf raid our battery fired around 110 *Gruppen*. During the raids on Krefeld, Mülheim, Gelsenkirchen and Köln our battery remained on the periphery. Only during the Solingen and Wuppertal affairs did the Lancasters and Halifaxes come close enough to our guns, and we gave them as good as we could.

During these weeks I learned the exact locations at night of cities in the Ruhr and the Rhineland. "What burns there?" "Duisburg." "There?" "Essen." "There?" "Köln." "And there?" "Dortmund." Fire is not just fire. Like snowflakes, each fire is different from others. To a *Flakhelfer*, standing by himself, watching on in silence as the red glows on the horizon or close by painted the clouds, caused an unspeakable sorrow in the heart.

The nightly raids did not end after these weeks. They only diminished a little, at least for a while. I had learned things I had never dreamed of or wanted to learn, gained knowledge I would never have any use for later, if I made it that far. These were fleeting thoughts. On July 3, I was granted a furlough for the weekend. The other kids on Bertha had been ahead of me. They had each gotten two days off because I had learned to fill in. On that Saturday morning I put on my dress uniform for the first time. To get to my parents' place I had to use a bus service that skirted the eastern edge of the city. Streetcar connections through the center were still obstructed.

First Furlough, July 3-4. It took me three hours to get to Gerresheim. I left the bus at the railroad station by the Glashütte factory main entrance and walked up

Heyestrasse toward our house. I felt awkward in the Hitler Youth uniform with the swastika armband. Those of us who had attended two KLV camps had fallen through the cracks in the system and, although registered in the *Jungvolk*, had not been inducted into the Hitler Youth. But here I was, wearing the uniform. I hoped that people who knew me and saw me would recognize the small black triangle with the letters LH and the blue *Luftwaffe* eagle over my right breast pocket that identified me as *Flakhelfer*, not as a Hitler Youth.

This particular section of Gerresheim had a history unique in Düsseldorf but similar to that of many cities in the Ruhr region. There, to serve the development of heavy industry, coal mines and steel mills, many thousands of workers, usually accompanied by their families, were brought in from the East, from East Prussia, the Baltic states, Poland, even Western Russia. The same happened in Gerresheim after a railway company built a railroad, in 1838, that connected Düsseldorf with the twin cities of Wuppertal-Elberfeld 50 kilometers to the east. This railroad, the first in Western Germany, bypassed the old Gerresheim and planted a station outside, "on the green meadow." In 1864 a glass factory was started next to it. Highly skilled workers were needed, because bottles and other objects were blown by mouth, single piece by single piece. The founder of the factory, Ferdinand Heye, recruited glass blowers from all over Eastern Europe. He paid travel expenses for workers and their families and offered rent- free housing in specially built brick masonry housing complexes grouped around the factory and the railroad station. The number of the polyglot, truly international body of workers reached 2,800 in 1890. The Gerresheim glass works were considered at the time the largest bottle manufacturer in the world.

But in 1890 the first machine was installed. Over the following years more and more machines were set up that made the old work force of craftsmen obsolete. Poverty of the unemployed, social decay and political unrest were the result. Police were brought in to evict the jobless from factory-owned housing. A great strike began in 1901 and lasted years. Social strife continued to 1914 and reached a higher level of intensity 1918, when the First World War ended. This part of Gerresheim had always been Socialist in political terms. After 1918, when the radical wing of the German Social Democratic Party broke away to form the KPD (Communist Party of Germany), most of the Socialists in the blue-collar part of Gerresheim joined.

My family had played a part in the unfolding of these events. My father's father had come from East Prussia in the 1880s and worked in the glass factory until he was evicted as an unremitting trade union organizer. He was not only kicked out of the factory, an order for his arrest was issued. He left the country with his wife. My father's oldest sister, Anna, was born in Belgium, a second sister, Martha, was born in France, and my father was born in Milan, Italy. Because of his unrepentant trade union and Socialist activities my grandfather and his family were expelled from these countries too. His wife finally fled the status of a penniless refugee and returned to Gerresheim into the protection of her brother. He held a senior position in the glass factory. Thus the three children grew up in the household of a bachelor uncle who despised his brother-in-law and treated the children with suspicion and neglect. My grandfather returned once secretly to Gerresheim. When his wife refused to see him, he met with the children. He told them that he would immigrate to America and would send them money to follow them there "on a big steamship." My father was four years old at the time of that meeting in 1899. This was the last time they saw my grandfather. Later, the children remembered, letters arrived from the US, but their mother destroyed them all and never said what their father had written or sent.

Despite, or perhaps because of his uncle's spiteful behavior, my father followed his lost father's political conviction and became a Social Democrat (the party later outlawed by the Nazi government). Because of his painful personal experience, my father was never active in politics. After the First World War and after recovering from a near fatal chest wound he received in Flanders, my father joined the machine shop of the Heye factory where he later became its head (*Werkmeister*).

During the rise of the Nazi party, lower Gerresheim, like the Ruhr area, was a Communist stronghold in Western Germany. Even before the Nazi takeover, Brownshirts (SA) were trucked in and fought street battles with local Communist commandos. I was an eyewitness to some of these as a boy five and six years old. Immediately after the Nazi takeover, in 1933, prominent Communists in lower Gerresheim were rounded up by Brownshirts and police in two purges and sent to "concentration camps." It was a new term we learned. Fathers of some of my playmates were among the men arrested and carried away.

This, perhaps, explains why I was embarrassed to walk Heyestrasse in my *Flakhelfer* uniform. Most of the people in this area, although silenced, remained hostile to the Nazi government. Not far from our house I met the father of one of my old buddies, Mr. Shimshok. Never prominent in the party, still he had always been a staunch Communist. I knew him and his family well. His youngest son, Heinz, a few years older than I, had been one of my earliest friends. I had lost track of him once I started Rethel *Gymnasium* and later went into KLV. When I was younger, Heinz had often read stories to me and introduced me to a bunch of kids with whom I ran around until school became too demanding.

Mr. Shimshok eyed me curiously and with disappointment, maybe even disgust. It was not me. It was the uniform. With anger in his voice, he said, "Now they have made my Heinz *kaput* too." His son had been killed in action in Russia. He looked at my uniform, the swastika. Heinz had grown up in a Communist family and now Russian Communists had killed him. I felt ashamed of my uniform. Perhaps he thought that I had become a Nazi. He could not know that I hated the uniform, too. How could I tell him. We stood for a long moment in silence. What could I say? Finally I mumbled something and walked on. The brief meeting stayed in my memory, and my conscience.

My mother had not expected me. She threw her arms around me before she looked me over in my uniform. In her eyes I detected something similar to what 1 had seen in Mr. Shimshok's eyes. Nothing accusatory, but sadness, a fatalistic expression. I went to my room and changed into civilian clothes I had brought back from the battery, short pants and shirt. They felt familiar but odd. I sat with my mother until my father arrived from the factory. We heard the front door close and his slow steps coming up the stairs. His face lit up when he saw me. Since I wore civilian clothes, he did not seem to see me as different from when he had seen me last. For me, that was already a long time ago. My mother had prepared lunch and afterward we went into the garden and sat on a bench. We talked about the two recent air raids on Düsseldorf and I added a bit about the raids I had witnessed from a distance. I said little about the Reisholz battery. My mother was pleased that the boys who had been in Einsiedel were able to stay together. My father was convinced that the war was lost. When the Nazi government declared war on the United States, in December 1941, my father told my mother and me that Germany could not win. He knew from the First World War that American resources and the two million fresh soldiers it brought to France led to the German defeat. On that mild July Saturday we did not talk about it. But it clearly was on my parents' minds. Still fifteen years old, I could not be too serious all the time. I told them that I had adjusted well and that the people in the battery were pretty good people. I said nothing about the long hours at the gun and little about the shooting. My father knew pretty much what I was going through but kept silent so as not to further frighten my mother. She was already frightened enough. We spent a pleasant evening. Before we went to bed my mother asked whether I would go with them to church in the morning. I said yes.

The alarm came before midnight. While the sirens screamed we quickly dressed and went downstairs. I carried a book and my mother's little black leather suitcase! In the cellar, a room had been set aside as air raid shelter for us and the family that lived on the first floor – a husband and wife and a girl of eleven. They had arrived before us and occupied one of the two long benches in the room. We nodded to them and sat down. I had forgotten how it felt to be in a cellar and wait for a raid or the sirens' all-clear. It was obvious that this lengthy waiting in air raid shelters was very different from our waiting in gun revetments. In the latter, we stood in the open, able to see what was going on around us. In air raid shelters the people sat densely packed in closed spaces, the elderly and infirm next to children of all ages, their mothers, and men too old for the military, all listening for sounds that penetrated from the outside. I looked at the curved vaults of the cellar of the house and wondered how much weight they would stand in case of a direct hit. I felt uncomfortable, caged. I was sure I was not alone in this. Once I went up briefly with my father into the court outside the house. We saw no searchlights testing the sky and heard no artillery fire. The night was still and clear. Later we learned that Köln had once again been hit that night.

In the morning we walked to St. Margaretha Basilica in the old part of Gerresheim for the 10 P.M. High Mass. The church, built in the 13th century in the Rhenish mixed Gothic-Romanic architectural style, was undamaged but for a few blown windows and scratches on its façade from bomb fragments. Three houses near the church were burned out. The pews were filled with worshippers. My mother found a place to sit but my father and I stood in the back. I had celebrated my First Holy Communion here when I was ten years old. I looked at the remaining windows high in the walls, with their colorful, stained glass, and their motifs, the figures of saints. The organ above us sounded with might, performing a Bach oratorio.

I knew the ritual but felt distant. The pastor gave a sermon from the pulpit, trying to be uplifting. Before communion the pastor read the names of six or seven members of the congregation who had recently died in combat. With the names he gave the locations where they had died. He read place names in Russia I had not heard before, Orel, Bjelgorod, and others. They had died, the pastor said, "Für Führer, Volk und Vaterland" (for the Führer, the People, and the Fatherland). After this he led the congregation in prayer for the Führer, Volk und Vaterland. This practice was repeated at every Catholic and Protestant church in Germany in every Sunday mass. I looked at my father. He stared ahead. I knew how he felt about the betrayal of the people by the Catholic Church hierarchy when it actively supported the chancellorship of Hitler that made him head of the new government. Like many others that Sunday, my mother went to receive Holy Communion. My father did not. Neither did I.

We spent a good day together. In the afternoon I took the .22 and briefly visited my hunting ground around the *Ruine*, looking for rabbits, not looking for rabbits. On this weekend I got closer to my parents than I had been a few weeks ago. Perhaps I had learned something in between. There was no alarm during the night. Early in the morning I got back into my uniform and left for Reisholz.

School Again, July 5. At 2nd Battery Headquarters I checked in from furlough. I was informed by the sergeant-major that school would be held in the mess hall after lunch if the scheduled teacher from our *gymnasium* was able to come. In our shack I changed into fatigues and went to Bertha. Only the three boys were present. The gun chief and K 3 seemed to have other obligations, and the Russians were laboring elsewhere. We talked and did some routine work in the revetment. We wondered whether class would actually happen. For us latecomers it would be a first time experience, for the others it meant a resumption after an interruption of 25 days caused by the Düsseldorf raids.

After lunch I spent the remaining time of the midday break with anticipation. At 1300 hours we were still waiting in the mess hall. When the teacher came, it was Dr. Peltzer, one of the Latin and History instructors from our school. In his early sixties, he was a warm and cordial man with a reputation of being soft on students. To his face, we called him by his title, but in general usage, to generations of students, he was Pedi. He knew his nickname and savored it because it meant students were fond of him. He was neither a member of the Nazi party nor of one of its organizations. In the recent past, during the many Nazi celebrations at our school, we were forced to wear uniforms. He and a few other teachers stood in civilian clothes while some of the teachers proudly wore their brown SA or black SS uniforms.

It felt like we had not seen him for a long time, although it had been only half a year. He looked drawn. We of the Einsiedel group stepped forward and reintroduced ourselves. He remembered us. He smiled. We felt sorry for him, as I was sure he felt sorry for us. He added our names to the roster of students. We took our seats. We were 35 or 36 boys from Rethel in the room. He told us latecomers what the others already knew: that he continued to teach Latin but had dropped History. He felt that Latin was more important to us now than History, because every student needed the *Grosse Latinum* (six years of Latin) to be able to enrol in a university. He knew, and we knew, that our learning had already been severely handicapped. Those of us who had been in Bad Einsiedel had not had Latin for almost half a year.

The teacher in Pedi prevailed. He gently led all of us back to the language of Gaius Julius Caesar's Gallic Wars, the old stand-by in Latin courses in all secondary education schools. Virtually every student had hated that text but never escaped from it. Now, in the Reisholz setting, Caesar' reflections on his war with Celtic and Germanic tribes seemed absurd, but we grudgingly agreed that for our welfare and misty future we should make an effort to understand them. Slowly, we found our way back into the intricacies of the ancient language.

After one and a half hours our next teacher arrived and Pedi took his leave. This was Wallerich, the mathematics teacher. He had no nickname because we did not know him well. He had been a teacher in Lessing *Gymnasium*, not our school. Those of us who had been in the KLV camp in Bad Spindelmühle in 1942 remembered him from that time. He was more impersonal than Pedi, a man with a dry humor and a good heart. We came to learn that he cared very much for us. He tried to make complex mathematics understandable to us in spite of the abysmal conditions we and he suffered. He was very good in his field but he never talked down to us. He tried to inform us about the logic of mathematics, the importance of thinking clearly, advising us to give ourselves to this fundamental, interdisciplinary tool of all sciences. He was gentle, hopeful. I don't think he expected much of us, and he was right. But he tried, and never disparaged our failures. From tiny gestures, the rising of eyebrows at specific moments or a slight shaking of his head, we recognized that he despised the system under which we were all forced to operate. In the Nazi state, even such small indications of disagreement with official policy was considered traitorous. He had to be careful. His allegiance was to us, and we honored him for that.

Like Pedi, he gave us homework to do. Both of them tried to show us we were still students, kids, that we still had a future when this period of the gun was over.

Both remained fixtures in our lives for the time we were in Reisholz. As long as the English continued to fly at night, only a direct raid on Düsseldorf prevented them from coming to us. They were always on time. Things changed after the middle of August 1943, when American *Viermots* began to make themselves felt in and around our area in extensive daylight raids. After that, there were many days when the alarm sounded during school sessions in the mess hall and we had to run to man the guns leaving our teachers behind in hopeless confusion. Once or twice Pedi followed us and took refuge in a trench below the Anton gun revetment.

Under these conditions school was a nearly impossible task. The teachers tried to make something of it and so did we. We had lost out on almost everything kids our age in normal times had access to and were able to experience. We knew that. We also knew we would have to make up later what we lost, including learning, if we made it to later. Despite everything we still thought we would. Sometimes, we came to regard our school sessions as an intermission from our daily and nightly activities, a breath of another world, perhaps a promise.

I wondered where those teachers from our school had gone who appeared in the SA and SS uniforms in Nazi festivities in times past. For instance, the authoritarian director of Rethel *Gymnasium*, Herr Budde. He was an SS man of Wallerich's age, but never showed up at the battery. The younger Nazi teachers were probably in military service, but what about the older ones? Had they been freed from work in the battery and rewarded by the party with easier jobs elsewhere, far from danger?

Life Becomes Routine. After the first weeks in Reisholz, we of the Einsiedel bunch settled in as well as the others who had been called up in February. A month ago, they had already been rewarded the *Flakkampfabzeichen.* It testified that they had served at the gun during the "kill" of eight enemy aircraft with which the Reisholz battery had been credited since their arrival. The medal, made of silvery metal, featured an oval wreath of oak leaves with an eagle on top holding a swastika. An 8.8cm gun inside the wreath pointed to the right at an angle of 45 degrees.

Our lives centred on three locations that defined our situation: the shack where we lived, the gun revetment, and the mess hall. The mess hall was the place where we had lunch with the battery personnel, where we picked up our breakfast and supper rations and where we had school three afternoons a week if the teachers could make it. The gun revetment was where we spent much time with the crew, hours many a night, and later, many hours during daytime raids, too. Much of our time was routine work, and much of the time we waited for what came or didn't come. When it came it was usually furious. Much was simply boring. The shack was the place where the six of us slept at night when we weren't on duty, where we ate together, did homework together, and spent our leisure time together. There was no place to go elsewhere. We had to stay near our gun, ready to answer the alarm call. So we became even closer than we had in Bad Einsiedel. We joked a lot and played tricks on each other, perhaps as a relief. There was no amusement for us there. We had to make it for ourselves.

My diary recalls important events that took place around us and elsewhere. Four days after my first furlough, Köln, was bombed again during the night of July 8-9, Gelsenkirchen again on July 10-11, Aachen on July 13-14. And Essen again on July 25-26. We did quite a bit of shooting during the Köln and Aachen raids. After the Essen raid we got to the English bomber stream as it came by after swinging around on its return. During these actions, as earlier, and during the time that followed, we four *Flakhelfer* on Bertha switched K 1, K 2 and K 6 positions between us constantly. It appears that I had become proficient at each.

The Essen raid had been a disaster for the Essen Flak. For the first time in the Ruhr area, English Pathfinders dropped a profusion of tinfoil strips that rendered the Flak radar system useless. The batteries were unable to fire at recognized targets. They could only hang a curtain of barrages in front of the incoming formations. Under these conditions the number of *Viermots* brought down was minimal.

In Russia a major German offensive called "Zitadelle" (the Kursk battle) had stalled, then was broken off when Allied forces landed on Sicily on July 10. We heard about it over the radio and read about it in newspapers. That was bad news, but it happened far away. What truly shocked us were the raids on Hamburg. They lasted from July 24 to July 30 – a "round the clock bombing" by English *Viermots* at night and American *Viermots* during the day. A firestorm was created that killed about 50,000 people. Reading about it left us with a doomsday feeling. This had been the worst attack on a single German city so far. Over Hamburg the English had used tinfoil strips for the first time in the war and had rendered the Flak impotent. But the Americans had bombed in daylight. They should have been targeted by optical fire control instruments called "*Kommando-Gerät 40*"(Command Device 40), but the planes had still gotten through. We wondered about German fighter planes. We had specialized nightfighters. The Me 109s and Fw 190s were supposed to protect us in daytime. Where were they?

We thought about this, but not deeply. There were a lot of experts somewhere who were supposed to take care of it. We did what we could when the bombers came to us. We were but little cogs in the apparatus. We felt confidence in ourselves at least. What concerned me at this time most was my sixteenth birthday coming on July 31, a Saturday, and that my request for a weekend furlough had been granted.

But on the night of July 30-31 (Friday to Saturday), the Royal Air Force attacked Remscheid, a mere 30 kilometers southeast of Düsseldorf. The bomber stream flew by us close enough that we hit it on the way in and, again, some of their formations on the way out. We fired many *Gruppen* that night during two different periods. I got back to our shack about 0225 in the morning. Because of my birthday, Corporal Tylia exempted me from helping to refill the ammo bunkers in the Bertha wall. After I left the battery on Saturday morning for the trip home, I took the swastika armband off. That had become a widely observed practice among *Flakhelfer*. On my first furlough I had not yet dared to do this. I boarded a bus, then, exhausted, fell asleep.

A Birthday, July 31. I had promised my parents I would be back for my birthday. It was accepted by the battery chief that boys were given furlough on such occasions. My mother was expecting me. I quickly changed into civilian clothes. My father arrived from the factory at noon. It was a sunny day and the dining room was filled with light. The day before, my father had bought a rabbit from an older man in the machine shop who raised them as meat animals. Dinner was a delight: rabbit roast, salad from the garden, fresh fruit from the *mirabellen* tree and a vanilla pudding for dessert. Even a glass of wine. Next to my plate was a package wrapped in colorful paper. I opened it to find a five volume edition of Friedrich Hölderlin's *Werke*, published by Eugen Diederichs in Jena in 1924. He was one of Germany's greatest lyric poets (1770-1843). I had always loved his poetry and already owned one of his books, *Diotima*. Here were the complete works. I was surprised and moved. My parents had gotten them from a second-hand book dealer. I still have this edition today.

My mother had also gotten four books for me that I wanted to take to Reisholz. They were from the *Volksbücherei*, the large city-owned and city-run public library housed in the main building of the elementary school Unter den Eichen where I had been a student for four years before I could enrol in Rethel *Gymnasium*. I had given my mother a list of books on my last furlough and asked her to talk to the librarian, Miss Jonen. I enquired about Miss Jonen.

My mother shrugged. "She is all right," she said "she asked about you. "

I remembered how I met her. The first time I went through the huge double doors of the library and up the four stairs to the great room I was awed. To the left was a long counter behind which a stern-looking librarian, the master of the magic mountain of books, held sway, giving reluctantly of her treasures. Straight ahead was a stand with newly arrived books, not yet numbered and registered, and to the right was a wide reading room with journals, newspapers, encyclopedias, and the like. I gathered my courage and joined the short line of devotees waiting to approach the master. I was the only child there. In front of the librarian, spread over the counter, were wooden boxes that held thousands of index cards, one for each book on the shelves.

From the high stand behind the counter she glanced, suspiciously, I thought, down at me, a little crumb below her, far below her. She asked what I wanted. I stuttered something like, "Books to read." She sadly shook her head. "How old are you?" she asked.

"Seven," I said.

After she asked whether I could read, and I said yes, she told me I needed a letter from my teacher and my parents. If I got these, she would help me filling out a library card with my name. She warned me that I could only get one book at a time, that I should never lend it to anyone else, that I should return it undamaged before the expiration date and that it cost 10 *Pfennige* for a total of 20 books. When she was through she smiled warmly, hopefully.

Her name was Miss Jonen. She was a spinster whose world was in books. She became my guide into this world. From my seventh year on I was a regular patron of this library, my visits only interrupted by the KLV camps. Back in Düsseldorf, I intended to continue getting books there and take them with me to Reisholz. Because I could only get furlough over weekends, when the library was closed, my mother became my go- between.

The books Miss Jonen started me on in 1934 were on the animal world and on American Indians. Of the books on animals of this period, I remember those written by Ernest Thompson Seton and Scandinavian authors, such as Bengt Berg, Egon von Kapherr, Fleuron and Foenhus. Among books on American Indians, she introduced me to the Leatherstocking Tales of J.F. Cooper and to the Fritz Steuben series on Tecumseh, the Shawnee chief. This was my beginning.

On that Saturday of my 16th birthday, my parents and I had a good day in the house and the garden. I helped to pick berries and ripe fruit. I was sorry that I could not be around to pick the fruit trees and for the heavier work.

There was no air raid alarm during the night. Through the open window I listened again to the melodious songs of nightingales, familiar magical sounds from a time that seemed lost, evoking memories of peace and beauty.

My mother asked about Reisholz but I said little. My father understood. He did not press me. Both were happy that I was with them.

In the morning they went to church but I took the .22 and went to the *Ruine.* I got two rabbits before they came back. I was not good at skinning but I managed. My mother did the rest. I was glad to leave something useful behind before I had to leave.

We had a good Sunday together. I didn't go anywhere. There were movie theaters close by and in the city, but I wasn't interested. I enjoyed the quiet of the old house, the garden, the green jumble beyond. I felt at ease. I knew my parents watched me, seeing perhaps certain changes in me including a more sober frame of mind. Perhaps that was so, but I still was a kid, sometimes serious, sometimes playful, able to switch from one emotion to the other not really knowing

I left early, taking Hölderlin and the library books with me. Becoming sixteen years of age did not seem to have been a particularly significant event. Not in my mind. Not with how our lives would continue. But I was pleased. I had made my parents happy.

Visitors from Grandfather's Land, August 12. School in the mess hall on Monday, Tuesday and Wednesday afternoons went smoothly for the next few weeks, without disruptions. The Royal Air Force flew attacks elsewhere, outside our area. Although we had to man the guns twice on successive nights, August 9-10, when Mannheim was hit, and August 10-11, when it was Nürnberg's turn. We only saw action after the Mannheim raid, when the returning bomber stream passed within our range.

I learned something about the personnel makeup of the Reisholz *Grosskampfbatterie*. It seemed there was a total of about 55 *Flakhelfer* in both the *Geschütz-Staffel* and *Mess-Staffel*, some 50 soldiers (including two officers, a Captain and a Lieutenant) in the Geschütz- Staffel, *Mess-Staffel*, *Tross-Staffel* and the searchlight section, six *Flakhelferinnen* (girls in uniform who worked in Battery Headquarters and in the *Mess-Staffel*), and about 50 Russian *Hiwis*. The Russians worked either as ammunition gunners or in the *Tross-Staffel* that included kitchen personnel.

This arrangement was probably average for an 8.8cm battery of twelve guns from early 1943 on when night raids (Royal Air Force) and day raids (US Air Force) on industrial installations and open German cities dramatically increased. Within batteries, personnel numbers probably fluctuated over time.

We were told that the anti-aircraft defenses of Düsseldorf consisted of seven batteries of heavy flak, two batteries of light flak. News from the war continued to be bad. In Russia, German troops were on the defensive, losing ground. On August 8 our forces had abandoned Sicily and begun retreating through Calabria. We never talked much about it.

There was a rumor afloat about the development of German "wonder weapons" that would change the course of the war in our favor. Many people believed it.

The rumor was fanned by hope, the hope that something better could happen after all. We in our shack in Reisholz tried to believe in it, too. But I remembered my father had said to my mother and me that he believed the war was lost. This I never told anyone. It was too dangerous. If such a statement was brought to the attention of authorities, the speaker would be considered a traitor and punished severely. Was my father wrong? How could he know that the secret weapons would not do what the government said they would?

My mother's older brother, Peter, first a member of a Communist veteran's organization, then a devoted Nazi, had whispered about these weapons already on the eve of the war. He had found work in the Rheinmetall weapons factory in Düsseldorf and pretended to know a great deal. When the factory was destroyed by English bombing in 1942, it was put back in production somewhere in Saxony. We had not seen him since. If he already knew before the war, where were these new, horrific weapons? Was it just a planted story? Was my father right?

I remembered a family outing in which my father made some critical remarks. My uncle threatened to report him if he continued to find fault with the "Führer." On the way back to our home I remember my mother saying, "This is getting dangerous. Either we don't see them anymore or we don't talk about politics anymore." We rarely saw my uncle and aunt after that.

The main event during early August was the first appearance of American *Viermots* in our area. It happened on August 12 in the early afternoon, a sunny day with light clouds overhead. We stood by the gun when reports came in that American bombers approached the Ruhr and were attacking Recklinghausen. We saw nothing but a thin cloud of smoke far to the north. We waited but nothing else happened. Then came a report from the *Mess-Staffel* that a second fleet of American bombers approached from the southeast.

First, swarms of our Me 109 fighter planes passed over, carrying drop tanks under their bellies, rushing northeast for a rendezvous over the Ruhr. Then we heard heavy anti-aircraft fire to the southeast. "Leading enemy formations over Solingen, flying north," Corporal Tylia laconically repeated the message from fire control. Solingen was only fourteen kilometers southeast of us. Over the rumble of gunfire and the staccato of exploding shells we heard another sound we had heard before, the steady growl caused by the engines of many heavy planes, *Viermots, Dicke Autos* (fat cars), as we sometimes called them. And then we saw them through breaks in the white clouds: a *Pulk*, "box," of some twenty to 30 planes, flying close together, surrounded by puff balls thrown at them by heavy Flak. We recognized them immediately by the sloping shark fins of the rudders.

These were B 17 Fortresses, large, silvery birds shining in the sun. They looked magnificent. The first *Pulk* passed. Keeping its distance, the second came up, following the same route, undeterred by the puffs that enveloped them. And another. And another. We watched, amazed, but also with a feeling of dread. The length of the stream of Fortresses was perhaps 100 kilometers long. We counted nine or ten *Pulks*.

We watched the last of them disappear. We had remained onlookers, eyewitnesses to the opening stage of a deadly play that would create havoc beyond our view.

I thought about my grandfather who had gone to America, the last place where he could live his life without being hunted by police. Had my father been able to join him there, and had I been born a few years earlier, could I have been in one of those silver birds? And what about our relatives from Solingen? Two couples had immigrated to America after the Great War. They lived in New Jersey and had come to us on a visit in 1937. Between them, they had two sons older than me. Could one or both of them be up there now?

That evening, we were informed that two groups of American *Viermots* had attacked the Ruhr, one from the northwest, the other from the south – the one we had seen. They had bombed Bochum, Recklinghausen and Gelsenkirchen. Some 25 Fortresses were shot down by fighters and Flak.

Two days later I went on furlough again. It was Ferdi's turn, too. On Sunday we went to see a movie in a city theater, a revue with Marika Röck in the lead role. She was a famous dancer and singer, a delight to look at, even for kids like us.

First Date. There were two false alarms during the next nights. We waited in readiness but sat huddled in the narrow bunker in the revetment because of a pelting rain. The Royal Air Force did not come near us. The English had introduced spoof raids. They sent Mosquitoes ahead that dropped *Christbäume* over a target to draw German nightfighters, then attacked elsewhere. We waited for hours but nothing happened. The real thing came early enough, on the night of August 22-23.

The Royal Air Force had flown another faint past the Ruhr but circled back and once again attacked Solingen, Düsseldorf and Leverkusen. First it appeared to be another false alarm night but then it turned out that bombers were coming in from the east. After we heard the anti-aircraft fire from Solingen and the sound of heavy bombing, we realized we might be in for it too. The sky was closed with a thick cloud cover and rain came down hard. We stood in readiness by the gun, wearing our steel helmets and heavy overcoats. The overcoats were too large for our slight figures but offered good protection, not only against the normal rain, but also against shell fragments raining down. When our targets were directly above us, which happened sometimes, the clatter of shell fragments falling around us was like bursts of hail. On that night, due to the heavy cloud cover, many searchlights pointed straight up. Their light bluish beams in the *Mattscheibe* position created the *Leichentuch* effect in the clouds. Thus our night-fighters, flying above the bombers, were able to see the shadows of the *Viermots* against the *Leichentuch* and could direct Flak barrage fire if our battery radar was hampered. They could also pursue targets themselves.

It did not take long before *Christbäume* in red and green drifted down through the clouds, marking an area close to us in the southwestern part of the city. First to fire was a 10.5cm battery to the west of us, at Himmelgeist. Other heavies, 10.5 and 12.8cm guns all around opened up. Then it was our turn. As the roar of the bomber stream passed over us, we fired *Gruppe* after *Gruppe*. We followed the enemy formations coming in, covering them nearly straight up, and switching to the next formations as they approached. I was K 6 that night, bent over the fuse setting machine, trying to be oblivious to the noise around us, the crashing of the gun, the inferno in the sky above us, and the earth-shattering impact of exploding block busters. The attack did not last more than twenty minutes but these were very long minutes. When it was over and I could look around, I saw a number of blazing fires to the northwest of us, growing, some merging, coloring the clouds. We wondered whether the Henkel Chemical Factory had been the target. If that was the case the bombers had missed and instead torched residential districts again. During the time I served as *Flakhelfer* in Reisholz, Henkel Chemical was never bombed although residential districts around the factory and beyond were destroyed.

Some bombs had fallen close to 1st Battery in the field of rye, but no damage was done. We stood in the rain, watching helplessly. Civilian fire-fighting trucks and Red Cross units rushed up on the road to the west of us, speeding toward the impact zone. Now they would be coming from all of the neighboring towns and cities, an effective cooperation established among the hard-hit centers of the Ruhr and the Rhineland.

In the morning the *Geschütz-Staffel* personnel and all the *Hiwis* worked to remove empty shell cases and refill the ammo bunkers in the revetments. School was suspended. Our teachers could not get to us. In the afternoon Thei took me aside.

He was with gun Dora and had been on furlough in Gerresheim over the weekend. On Sunday he had met a girl who lived in his neighborhood. Her name was Edith. He had known her for years but never spoken to her. She went to Augusta Victoria *Gymnasium* and had taken the same tram at the same time and station Thei took it to Rethel. That was so in the past. When he saw her on Sunday, he approached her. They talked. They agreed to meet on the Saturday of his next furlough, September 4. She said she would bring a girl friend and asked whether he had a friend he could bring, too. He told her he would. Then he told me, "You must come with me on that Saturday. I need you. She won't see me without her girl friend. And the girl friend expects me to bring a friend. That's you."

I was surprised. I didn't know what to say. Finally I said, "My furlough is a weekend before that."

"Yes," Thei said. "Just take it a week later." He looked hopeful. I didn't know Edith. Perhaps I had seen her on the tram also. I had no idea what she looked like. I liked Marika Röck from the movies, an exciting woman, but I was a boy. KLV had not been helpful to us for understanding girls, nor had Reisholz. We had been left out. I told him that I would write a letter to tell my parents that I would come a week later. At Bertha I had to switch with one of the boys. So it was decided. The meeting with the girls was to be on the designated day, September 4.

We had only one shooting affair before that, on the night of August 30- 31. The English attacked Mönchen-Gladbach, a city eighteen kilometers straight west of Düsseldorf without important industry. Much of the city was laid low, nevertheless. We got some of the bombers before they swung around for home.

Elinor. She was sixteen also, two months older than I. She was slender with straight legs and small breasts under her dress. An oval face framed by brown hair, brown eyes. Her eyes were inquisitive, observing, questioning. She was quite shy, not more so than I. She lived on Keldenichstrasse about two blocks down from Thei's parents' place.

On that early Saturday evening I walked the one kilometer from my parents' house to meet Thei on Keldenichstrasse. Edith was already waiting there with him. A dark-haired girl almost seventeen, she was outgoing, with an easy laugh. She was well-built, with dark, bemused eyes. She and Elinor attended the same school, the same class.

They were good friends. After I was introduced we set out for Elinor. We walked the two blocks to her house and Edith went to the door to ring the bell.

That seemed to be the agreed-upon sign. But Elinor, on the second floor, probably had watched us through the window, perhaps with her parents. I don't remember how I felt. I don't think excited. Curious, perhaps, and a little awkward, like a conspirator. After all, this arrangement had been made without any involvement on my part. It did not take long before Elinor came through the door.

It seemed she felt awkward too. That was something we had in common, although it would not help us much. Extroverted Edith took charge of the situation, and after introducing us to each other, suggested we walk together in the direction of the Germania movie theater. We walked in a row, Edith doing the talking. I cast self-conscious looks sideways at Elinor. She was aware of my glances but didn't look back. It was the first time I ever walked with a girl. I didn't know what to say and neither did she. We were both uncomfortable. Edith kept talking, with Thei sometimes getting in too. He was more comfortable in this situation than I, easier in the presence of girls. He appeared pretty smooth while I felt like a clod. He must have had some experiences in this field that I didn't. So it went for a while. I didn't like small talk and did not try to join in. I thought that it was getting worse for me by the minute. Here was a pretty, healthy girl beside me and I didn't know what to do. Finally she asked me a question. That broke the ice a little.

It was a question about school, and what I was reading. There I had something to say, and we began a conversation. When we got to the movie theater the show had already started. So we continued walking, Thei and Edith going ahead, Elinor and I following a dozen steps behind.

This became pretty much the rule for the next few months when Thei and I had furloughs together. We did a lot of walking with the girls in the evenings, in the dark. Because the English came later at night, we were pretty safe. There was nothing else to do, no place we could have gone. We were too young for visiting bars. Cafés and shops were closed at that time. We went to the movies a few times. We rarely talked about our duties at Reisholz and never about the war. Thei had an older brother in the *Heer*, serving in Russia. Sometimes Thei and I wore our dress uniforms to our rendezvous, but without the swastika armbands. I never met Elinor's parents and she never met mine. We never considered it. Our relationship never became intimate. I kissed her twice, our lips touching briefly. It felt good, but led to nothing more. We did write letters to each other. She wrote on pale blue, silky paper that smelled of perfume. It smelled good. We wrote a little about love in a clumsy, searching way.

Her father was too old for military service. He owned a small factory that produced tins with a special chocolate mixture as energy food for the *Luftwaffe*.

Her parents must have been strict because Elinor could never slip me a precious tin. It didn't matter.

She was the first girl I felt somewhat close to. After three months, in December 1943, she and her mother were resettled by her father in a small town in the Taunus Mountains. It was for their safety because of continuing air raids in our area. For a few weeks we continued exchanging letters, then she stopped. She probably saw no future in our timid relationship. I guessed she was right. I did not blame her, although I still felt a degree of loss. Perhaps, I thought, she had found someone older and more mature than me. I hurt, though. I was competent enough in working the big gun, but not in dealing with a pretty girl.

The Sunday after that first meeting with Elinor I spent with my parents. Twice during the night the air raid alarm sounded. The first came at about 2400 hours. I got up and dressed quickly. I took a book with me. When I stepped into the corridor I did not have to wait for my parents. It had become routine for everyone under the threat of nightly raids to get ready fast. I grabbed my mother's little black leather suitcase and followed my parents down the stairs into the cellar. Our neighbors from the first floor came in at the same time, a husband and wife and their young daughter. We sat on benches and chairs in the narrow room set aside as a shelter. Faces looked tired and weary, listless, yet attentive, listening for portentous sounds from outside. We sat in silence. I turned to my book and read. After 45 minutes the sirens screamed the all-clear signal. The RAF had passed us by and gone elsewhere deeper into Germany. We slowly left with a few friendly words, a load lifted.

The second alarm came at 0130. Again we went to the bomb shelter in the cellar. Nothing happened for about 20 minutes. Then we heard the rumble of distant Flak fire from the south, the direction of Köln. It lasted for a little while and then the guns fell silent. The all-clear signal once again filled the air.

Next morning, when Thei and I arrived in Reisholz, we learned last night's English raids had visited the cities of Ludwigshafen and Mannheim, both on the upper Rhine, and had come close to the Bonn and Köln anti-aircraft guns on the way back.

A Sky full with Vapor Trails. On a sunny, cloudless day, September 6, as we readied for lunch, alarm bells called us to the guns. Pedi, our Latin teacher, had already arrived but it didn't look good for school. We stood around the gun, waiting for information. The time of the alarm was suspicious. A daytime raid meant that American bombers were on the way. Sirens to alarm the civilian population remained silent. The men on our gun, as usual, smoked cigarettes. The corporal wore headphones and microphone. When the command post called he reported the message to us. "Leading enemy formations over Calais, proceeding southeast." They would have to be Americans. The course could be a faint. If they continued on the same course they would pass perhaps 300 kilometers to the south of us. We had to wait to find out. No new information came for 35 minutes. Then, "Leading enemy formations north of Reims. Reims?" Tylia drily offered, "Perhaps it's München."

We stood or sat idle for nearly two hours, making small talk. Why were we still kept in readiness when the target was in southern Germany? No one asked the question aloud. Lunch and our Latin class had gone away. Did the command know what it was doing? Finally Tylia's headphones crackled, "Leading formations over the Rhine near Karlsruhe, continuing direction 4." Ten minutes later, "Heavy air raid on Stuttgart."

So. Another city. This was a large one, now a shadow of its former size like so many cities, our city included. The RAF had hit Stuttgart a dozen times or more already. Now a daytime raid? I could imagine what was going on there, but I didn't want to think about it. We had become numb to disasters, apathetic, locking our feelings away. On the guns, we did what was expected of us and did it well, not with enthusiasm, but with a degree of purpose and urgency.

Next we heard, "Bomber stream has turned north, direction 11." "They are coming down the Rhine," Tylia said. Forty-four minutes later we heard distant Flak fire to the south. "Leading formations west of Bonn." We waited another fifteen minutes and then we saw to the southwest, inexorably coming north parallel to us at a distance of fifteen kilometers, the first vapor trails of the American bomber boxes streaking the blue sky. One *Pulk* followed another, leaving ballooning white clouds behind. There were narrower vapor trails crisscrossing around the bombers, German fighter planes harassing and attacking the boxes. We stood and watched. It was like watching a movie. The bomber stream was on its way home but did not have an easy going. It had probably been under fighter attack off and on from the moment it crossed the French coast, and these might continue until it left the mainland. During one of the first deep penetrations of American *Viermots*, the Schweinfurt and Regensburg raids, August 17, 60 *Viermots* were shot down, mostly by Me 109 and Fw 190 fighters. The Stuttgart raid could have a similar ending. We saw two *Viermots* break formation and lose attitude, eventually disappearing from our sight.

The column of bomber boxes was about 100 kilometers long and took 30 minutes to pass. They left behind a sky filled with slowly dissolving vapor trails, and left us impressed with the power of these aircraft. Nazi leadership had said at the beginning of the war no enemy bomb would fall on German soil. Now it was obvious to everyone that the night over Germany belonged to the English, the day to the Americans. Nothing would change that. How did we feel watching from our gun revetment? Useless against these odds. But another night or day, we would shoot if we had the chance.

During the next two weeks the English bombed München once but did not come into our neck of the woods. The Americans didn't show either. Perhaps they needed a break too. We certainly did. In September we latecomers from Bad Einsiedel were summoned to 2nd Battery Headquarters where the lieutenant, our battery chief, handed each of us the *Flakkampfabzeichen* with a handshake and a brief smile. For the time we had served since our arrival, Reisholz *Grosskampfbatterie* had been credited with eight *Abschüsse*, kills of enemy aircraft. More than anything we were surprised. We stood in rank, fingering the unexpected medals, until the lieutenant discharged us with a nod. Ours was not a saluting outfit concerned about ceremony. We served in a combat battery.

I kept looking forward to my next furlough on the weekend of September 18-19. Elinor was on my mind.

Paul. We sat in the living room, my parents' faces sad and strained. "Paul has been killed in Italy," my father said. "Where?" I asked. He shrugged. "Somewhere south of Naples. Anna got the news two days ago." Anna was my father's sister. She and her husband, Konrad, had two sons, Willi and Paul, and a daughter, Annie. Willi had died in action in Russia. Now Paul was gone too.

I remembered my cousins fondly. Willi had been the introverted one, a tall, good- looking young man with a dry humor. Paul was the extrovert, a year older than Willi, a happy, fun-loving guy full of life, mischievous, bright. He was a lieutenant in a *Gebirgsjäger* Division when he married. It was before I went to Bad Einsiedel. My parents and I had attended the wedding in Gerresheim. His pretty young bride came from Berchtesgaden in the Bavarian Alps, where her parents owned a hotel. A nice, attractive couple. We had a very good time at the wedding. The war and Willi's absence, for at least that day, not forgotten but set aside, given over to a simple joyous event.

We sat in dark silence. There was more bad news. My father briefly related, what I, in our little, closed, tense world in Reisholz, was not aware of and not eager to learn. Italy had collapsed. A new Italian government had signed an armistice with the Western Allies. Our forces disarmed the Italian army, Mussolini's own people imprisoned him. German troops were withdrawing across Italy to a line north of Naples, Allied armies following on their heels.

We sat. What to say? Finally my mother ended the unease. "Let's go into the garden," she said. Among the trees and flowers we felt better. Another world still existed. The beauty we saw around us was a reflection of it.

In the evening I met with Thei and the girls. We tried to see a movie in the Germania theater but the box office cashier refused us tickets because we were under eighteen. The movie might have had a nude or near nude scene, too dangerous for us to see. We spent the evening walking.

In the morning I went again to church with my parents for the high mass. This time the list of those fallen in combat from the St. Margaretha congregation included a new place name, Salerno. There were also two or three from Russia. The war wasn't over there, either. After lunch, as on my preceding Sunday furlough, I worked in the garden harvesting fruits and vegetables. I generally disliked this work but felt it necessary for me to do. My father could no longer do much physical labor. I could not leave it to my mother alone.

Bitter Autumn. According to my diary, the following three weeks, September 20 to October 8, were hard. The RAF once again stepped up its bombing campaign. Of these nineteen nights, only five (September 20, 21, 25, 26, October 6) didn't require us to stand-by or go into action. On these nights the following cities were bombed: Hannover, Mannheim, Ludwigshafen , Darmstadt, Braunschweig, Bochum, Hagen, München, Kassel, Frankfurt and Stuttgart. In addition, American daylight raids struck Frankfurt, Wiesbaden and Saarbrücken on October 4. This time we saw nothing of B 17 Fortresses or B 24 Liberators. We did a great deal of shooting during the raids on Bochum (September 23-24), and Hagen (October 1-2) and got into action when the English got close on their return from Mannheim and Darmstadt (September 23-24), München (October 2-3) and Frankfurt (October 4-5).

Because of the intensity of the English campaign and the probability of another attack on our city, furloughs were canceled for the weekend of October 2-3. Because of the many nights we spent by the guns we became physically and mentally exhausted. We kept asking the question why, to the RAF, civilian populations seemed appropriate targets as much as industrial and military installations. "Terror bombing," as it was called, confirmed to many that the Nazis were right at least in one claim. The Allies intended not only to win the war, but to destroy everything German. As we watched the cities burn around us it felt that way. When we kids worked the guns, we did not shoot for an ideology or a government. We shot for something immediate, direct and close by. We tried to protect, as best as we could, the civilians, including our parents, women, children, old people, crouching in bomb shelters and bunkers behind us.

Ferdi, Wenner, Hannes and I of our little group, and a number of other *Flakhelfer*, were granted furlough for the weekend of October 9-10. The battery chief must have thought that we needed it. Since Thei had not been allowed out, I could not see Elinor on that Saturday. Ferdi and I went in the afternoon to a movie in a downtown theater that stood among ruins and rubble but still functioned. We watched a heroic tale from the Seven Year's War. After the movie we went to one of the remaining cafés and had a cup of chicken broth before we took the tram home. Ferdi was worried about his brother, Otto, two years older than us, who served in a paratrooper division in Italy and was perhaps in the midst of fighting there.

I spent the evening with my parents. I returned the books from the *Volksbücherei* to my mother and collected four new ones she had gotten for me during the week. I mentioned that, on the information board in battery headquarters, we had seen an announcement by Military Command recommending *Flakhelfer* should apply for officer's careers in the armed services. Because the German officer corps was recruited mostly from graduates of secondary schools, the ad made sense. My parents felt that if I applied, and was accepted as a reserve officer candidate, I would be safe from the grasp of the *Waffen-SS*. They hounded boys like us to volunteer for the *Waffen-SS*, the military arm of the SS organization. This fear was common and justified. I agreed to apply.

Next day I worked again in the garden but took some time off to visit the green thickets around the *Ruine*. I took the .22 but saw no rabbits. No regrets. I didn't feel like killing anything. The wood of the rifle stock felt good in my hands, something sturdy, reliable, that I could handle comfortably. There was no alarm on these two nights.

Kleine Oma. Reporting back to 2nd Battery Headquarters, Ferdi and I filled out applications for reserve officer candidate for the *Heer*. This was duly registered in our papers, as was the earlier award of the *Flakkampfabzeichen*. German bureaucracy, civilian and military, never missed recording details. It took a few weeks, however, until our applications were formally accepted and confirmed. In order to meet with Elinor again I switched a furlough due me from October 23-24 to October 30-31 so I could go with Thei. It worked both ways – without me and Elinor he would not be able to see Edith.

During the following three weeks we stood-by twice during American daytime raids. On October 14, once again, Schweinfurt and the ball-bearing factories were hit, and on October 20, the Düren airfield, 45 kilometers southwest of our battery. We waited by the guns for hours but never saw a Viermot. We watched quite a few German fighter planes rushing southwest. That was all. There were three night alarms, but we only had a chance to shoot at formations of the RAF returning from an attack on Leipzig, deep in Eastern Germany (October 21-22). On that night the sky was clear. Three Lancasters were riding the cones of searchlights, allowing visual ranging. Two were brought down around Düsseldorf, one crashing close by, on the west bank of the Rhine, half a kilometer away.

The RAF attack on Kassel, October 22-23, was the worst since the Hamburg raids. The bomber stream, 150 kilometers long, flew in from the southwest of us, over Koblenz and Bonn. At 2200 hours we waited by the gun. It could be Düsseldorf again. At 2300 we listened to the endless thunder in the sky, but the fleet passed us without us getting a shot. An hour later we heard that it was Kassel's turn again. The newspaper reported two days later that the firestorm created by the bombers in Kassel killed ten thousand people. Excluding the Wednesday of the Düren raid, we had eight days of school, ranging from the Gallic Wars to the intricacies of math. On the Saturday afternoon of the furlough, October 30, Thei and I met with the girls. We went to the Germania theater and saw a silly, totally unrealistic, sentimental movie. We didn't care as long as it provided an antidote to the grim world out there. We were happy sitting together, feeling each other's presence. We took a long walk after that, Elinor and I, like Thei and Edith, arm in arm.

On Sunday morning I went with my parents to Erkrath, a little town at the opening of the Neandertal, three kilometers east of Gerresheim. We went to the cemetery with flowers for my grandmother's grave. The holiday of *Allerheiligen* (All Saints) was on the following Monday. It was custom in Germany to visit the graves of the dead on that day and place flowers in remembrance. Because I had to be back in Reisholz on Monday, we decided to go on Sunday.

It was a small grave with a headstone engraved with my grandmother's name. My mother cleared dead leaves away and placed the flowers we had brought in a metal vase. We lit a candle that would burn for 24 hours.

My grandmother. For the first six years of my life she was my guardian angel, my teacher, my inspiration, my guide into worlds distant and colorful and strange, my everything. I called her fondly. "kleine Oma," because of her small size. She was born in Erkrath on July 28, 1862. Her maiden name was Gertrud Kloft. She married Johann Kopp on September 30, 1889. My mother Maria Kopp, was born in Erkrath on October 12. 1896. She was the youngest of three children. A brother, Peter was two years older, a sister, Lisbeth, three. Their father died when my mother was two years old. He had been called up for army fall maneuvers and came back with pneumonia. It took his life within a few weeks. He had been the manager of the Erkrath railway station and my grandmother had to live with three small children on a modest pension from the railway company, the Rheinische Bahngesellschaft, and from the work she did from her house. These were years of hardship. She grew much of the food for the family in her large garden. When the children finished elementary school, they each learned a trade. My mother spent four years becoming a dressmaker. Afterward, she worked in a fashion house in Düsseldorf.

My mother met my father in 1922. He married my mother on October 15 1924. He worked in the Heye glass factory then, that had once evicted his father and, in many ways, had been a big part in shaping his life. My grandmother's left leg had been amputated due to an illness, so my parents moved into her home. I was born on July 31 1927, and I spent the first three years there under my grandmother's constant attention and care. In 1930 my parents and Kleine Oma moved to lower Gerresheim, where my father rented the larger part of a house across from the factory-owned library, well stocked with books. My grandmother had a prosthesis, but she had difficulty walking. In Gerresheim, as in Erkrath before, she rarely left the house. She spent almost all her time with me, an only child.

The two of us became frequent visitors to the library across the street. Lugging books from the library to our house and back was my mother's task. Kleine Oma opened the world of books for me. I learned that through books, one can travel anywhere, to the most distant, wonderful, and exotic places. One could hide in books. It was a valuable lesson. I found it life-saving later.

We would sit side by side, my grandmother showing me pictures and telling me about them, inventing stories. Later I understood that among the volumes she had gone through with me were those of the Theodore Roosevelt African Expedition where species were collected for American museums. There were a great many photographs of African plains game published there. She sat me on a cushion on the kitchen table as she sat on a chair before me while I held my arms around her. She would whisper stories into my ear. When she paused, my mother told me later, I would say, "Mehr, Oma, mehr." I could not yet speak well but I listened very well.

The stories she told me sank deep and did something there inside me that, many years later, came to the fore. I remember that she told me Sami stories of white reindeer and sleds and magicians and a sacred mountain, a mountain spirit called Hitzi. She told me many others. These were not the Brothers' Grimm or Hauff fairy tales; she told me those too, but where many of the others came from I do not know. She told me of Maya pyramids and lost Inca treasures, of ancient cities in the green jungle. These I somehow remember. But I have lost so many others – or have I?

She died on February 4. 1933. I was almost six years old. I was scared, befuddled, and uneasy for a long time. I could not understand that she would not come back. In the early mornings I listened for the tap-tap of her cane as she came down from the two rooms upstairs where she had lived. The familiar sounds signaling her arrival came no more.

Later, in elementary school, I was the first in class who could read, the first to enrol in the big library next to the school. That was my grandmother's legacy. She would have been smiling, wherever she was.

On that Sunday with my parents I knelt and touched the earth on her grave before we walked away. She had taught me that the world was a place of wonder, of miracles, of meaning, and for a long moment I remembered all that, remembered her face below the black stone inscribed with her name.

Düsseldorf Again. The expected attack on our city came during the night after All Saints, on November 2-3. The alarm bell woke us at 2200 hours. We took to the bunker in the Bertha gun revetment because of a drizzling rain. Tylia reported leading formations over Zeeland, the southern tip of Holland, 225 kilometers almost due west of us. If they aimed for the Ruhr or the Rhineland, they would arrive in less than an hour. Perhaps it was another faint? We took our stations after the bomber stream was passing Antwerp, continuing in direction 3. In the city the sirens screamed. Searchlights aimed their beams at the cloud cover. Tylia reported us ready to the command post. We waited. Finally, "Gun position 9." The faint sound of aircraft. The windows before the K 1, K 2 and K 6 lit up, command pointers began to move. "Covered." Flak started up west of the city. We heard the roar of many aircraft, closing in. Red light cascades, *Christbäume*, emerged over the city, slowly passing through the clouds. It was our turn, again.

Green *Christbäume* followed the red. The attack lasted about 25 minutes. The explosions of blockbusters roared even over the noise of our shooting. We fired well over a hundred rounds that night. The ground within the revetment filled with the clutter of empty brass cases. Only after the last of the bombers had vanished did we have a chance to breathe, to look around, to think. North of us we saw great blossoms of smoke against the bluish-white beams of the searchlights. There, three kilometers away, people had died. More were suffering. We, in our battery, had been spared again. Why, and for how long? The question left me with a queasy feeling in my stomach.

For us, the next two weeks were quiet ones. The RAF paused. Perhaps their crews were exhausted, too. They lost a bunch of aircraft every time they crossed into Germany to nightfighters and Flak. It did not deter them much. Their resources in men and material seemed inexhaustible. We had long regarded the English and their Commonwealth Allies, the Canadians, Australians and New Zealanders as tough and resilient in war. Their bomber squadrons were no exceptions. True, they dealt in death, but death cut into their formations, too. On average they lost somewhere between fifteen to 25 planes in a raid, sometimes more. Still, they kept coming. We never knew what they expected to gain from burning civilians in one city after another, and attacking the same targets again and again. If they thought the stricken population would buckle, they were mistaken. People living under the constant threat of death, with no chance to change it, were forced to accept it. When the sirens blared, people went into concrete bunkers, into tunnels dug into rises of the ground, and cellars. There they huddled and waited, suffering in silence. The general frame of mind of our people under such horror was apathy, resignation, impassivity. Soldiers on the battlefields fought on with desperation, more so because they knew what was happening to their families back home.

I saw it in my parents' eyes on my next furlough. November 13-14. I saw it in their expressions, their bearing. In lower Gerresheim a three story concrete bunker had been finished that no blockbuster would be able to penetrate. It was over half a kilometer from our house. My father had become a slow walker. If my parents tried to get there during an alarm they might not make it if Gerresheim was a target. So they stayed in the cellar of our home, hoping that the thick walls and the solid vault would protect them.

My father, always an introvert, looked drained and impassive. He was withdrawing within himself. He tried to be more positive because I had come and he did not want to burden me. Even trying was hard for him. My mother, always the optimistic, encouraging, practical one, tried to shift us into a more amiable mood. Eventually she succeeded because my father knew that gloom did us no good. And, after all, I had come on furlough.

At first I saw my parents' discomfort, their unhappiness, almost as an outsider. Although I lived under conditions similar to theirs, I had a different opinion about the overall situation. Strangely, the bombing and the killing had not yet made an impact on me as severe as it had on them. It must have been youthful ignorance on my part. I still saw, my buddies saw, some hope where my parents saw none. I realized that something was happening to them, changing them. For the first time in my life I felt sorry for them. For the first time after Einsiedel I felt the kind of closeness to them as I'd felt when I was a little boy. They were my parents and I knew I loved them. I didn't tell them and I carried my feelings to our Saturday evening meeting with the girls. Perhaps that was why I kissed Elinor then – an overwhelming sudden awareness that there is love despite grime and misery.

Fortresses. During the following two weeks there were only three days without a night alarm: November 15-16, 16-17, 21-22. During the other nights we spent many hours by the guns. The English had flown through and attacked away from our area: Berlin, four times, Ludwigshafen, twice, and Mannheim, Frankfurt and Stuttgart. The only exception was the raid on Leverkusen, November 19-20. This small town, home of the Bayer Werke, was just twenty kilometers to the southeast of us. That night we were heavily engaged and fired around 80 *Gruppen*. As so many times before, we could not prevent disaster. We glumly watched the sky redden. Twice during that time period we shot at Lancasters returning from one of the cities mentioned above. Often, the bomber stream flew in to the north of us and returned to England across the North Sea, where the planes were preyed upon by nightfighters. American daytime raids during these weeks focused on German coastal cities, such as Emden, Bremen, Wilhelmshafen. We were glad to be overlooked.

My furlough on November 27 and 28 was uneventful. For some reasons the girls were elsewhere, so I spent the whole time with my parents. We hardly mentioned the most recent attack on our city. The northern part of Düsseldorf had been hit again. Some bombs had fallen into the already devastated downtown area. They had severed a section of the surviving streetcar tracks among the rubble, one of the lifelines of the city.

We knew this would continue. There was not much to say about it. I spent some time again with the .22 on my old hunting ground near the *Ruine*, mainly to be by myself for a while.

Our first American raid came two days later, on the afternoon of November 30. The Fortresses came at a height of 5,000 meters (18.000 feet). We thought we were in for it. We saw the first of the combat boxes as they flew in from the northwest. The sky around them came alive with the puff balls of exploding shells. These were from guns of calibers heavier than ours, 12.8cm and 10.5cm, stationed on the other side of the city. The 8.8cm batteries joined in as the planes came closer. A little later they were in our range. My last look at them, before the command pointer in the K 2 position in front of me began moving, was not in awe, as before. This time I felt deadly fear. Here they were, coming for us. At English planes, we as gunners shot blind, in the dark. We only saw those planes in rare situations. The sky had to be clear, us out of range and watching as searchlights picked them up and made them visible. But here a whole fleet converged upon us in broad daylight. Still, the command pointer required my attention. I could do nothing but cover it with the position pointer. While Bertha roared and shook and empty cases clattered behind us, I listened for the terrible sounds of bombs coming down.

That sound never came. The Fortresses passed over us, enduring our fire, our anger, oblivious to our fear. They went by and did their part in the continuing obliteration of Solingen, the place my relatives had left to find a better life in America. So had many Germans from other towns and villages. Among them my grandfather. Now the American planes were doing during the day what the English did at night, killing civilians. I wondered what in Solingen was of military value. America had a good name in Germany. In the past she had always been a haven on the other side of the ocean. We felt angry and disappointed.

We shot a lot that day as their formations came, one after the other holding a steady course at the same operational height. After our guns became silent, we still saw the Solingen Flak fire. We heard the rumble of heavy carpet bombing as one *Pulk* after another unloaded on the city. And then they were gone, leaving their vapor trails behind them. Tylia told us that he had seen three *Viermots* going down.

The next American attack came the following day, December 1. This time Leverkusen was struck. The English had hit the town eleven nights earlier. We could see the bomber boxes clearly to the west, in a sky filled with vapor trails but out of our range. Something must have been left standing in Leverkusen, before this. We watched the long snake of planes passing by, dragging vapor trails and barely touched by anti-aircraft fire. It all seemed to happen in slow motion.

Over meals in our hut or in the mess hall, or during the time we met for class, we didn't talk about what was happening or what we were doing. Neither did the teachers. They kept silent. So did we. There was nothing to talk about. We went to the guns when we had to. We did what was expected of us. When it was over, we went back to our quarters. We had become stoic, impassive. During attacks we had no time to think about anything. We worked the machines. When we could, we cracked jokes and made fun of each other. We were not unhappy. I guess we had become as weird as the world we lived in. We still read books in our free time and did class work, the latter more out of necessity than for love of learning. School, although somewhat unreal in our world, at least distracted us from the other things we had to do.

My next furlough, December 11 to 12, was the last time I met with Elinor. She told me she and her mother would be leaving Gerresheim for a place her father had found for them in the south, away from any city. Although we had not been more than friends, it was a sad loss for me. She had been the first girl I had known, and I liked everything about her. We both knew that if our lives had not been overshadowed by the darkness around us things could have been different. Our relationship might have become closer, perhaps something precious. She gave me her new address, a village in the Taunus Mountains, and promised to write.

Ilya, Vassiliy, Piotr. They were three Russian soldiers who, as many others, had volunteered to serve in the German anti-aircraft. As volunteers they were called *Hiwis* (*Hilfswillige*, "willing to help"). We never called them *Hiwis*, we called them by their first names. They didn't call us by name but used the informal, personal "Du" instead of the formal "Sie," and our last names, the way we were addressed by commissioned and non-commissioned officers. Tylia was the exception; he called Paulchen "Du" and "Sie" at different times.

The three Russians were in their late twenties. Ilya was a high school teacher from Orenburg, near the southern edge of the Ural Mountains. Vassiliy was from Irkutsk, a city on Lake Baikal in Siberia. Piotr was from a village 300 kilometers south of Moscow. The three were our ammunition gunners. The K 5 and K 7 removed the shells from the ammo bunkers in the revetment walls and passed them to the K 4, who slipped them into the two receiving cups of the fuse setting machine worked by the K 6. We *Flakhelfer* rotated from the K 1 to the K 2 and the K 6 positions, but among the Russians, their positions, once established, remained the same. Vassiliy was the K 4, Ilya was K 5, Piotr was K 7. They had chosen these positions, and Tylia did not interfere. What mattered to him was that we were a smooth-working unit.

Of the three, Ilya spoke a little German, the other two only a few words or phrases. Ilya was a handsome, slender man who liked to laugh. Vassiliy was a strong, quiet man, with a broad face that showed features of the physical make-up of ethnic groups in his Siberian homeland. Piotr was a little shorter than the others, agile, with a sharp face and quick eyes.

We *Flakhelfer* had a good relationship with the three, I perhaps more than the other boys. I was curious about them, their backgrounds, where they came from. I was especially interested in Vassiliy. I was fascinated by Siberia. I had read some books about that vast, beautiful land and the original people there, hunters and reindeer herders. I had read about tigers and leopards and the Nanay people on the Amur River. I had read about gatherers of ginseng in the deep forests of Sichota Alin, who made gifts to the snow tiger, the Master of the taiga. And I had read a little about Koryak and the Evenks. I was eager to learn from Vassiliy. Ilya tried to translate. But Vassiliy did not understand what I was curious about, didn't know himself, or didn't want to speak about it. Perhaps I touched something that made him even more homesick. I gave up after a while. I didn't hold it against him.

There were both visible and invisible dividing lines between us that we could not breach. After all, we boys were German. They were Russian prisoners of war. At times we were able to forget. For instance, on many nights, when nothing happened, we stood by the revetment wall together and talked, or tried to talk. The three were friendly, but reserved. They were clearly homesick and worried about their future. They wondered if they ever would go home again. If Germany lost the war, which they thought likely then, they expected no mercy from Stalin for having served in the German war effort. If Germany should win, their future was still uncertain. In either case they would lose.

I talked with them about their fears out of earshot of the others at Bertha. They came to trust me, but there was nothing I could do. I was not the master of my own life, nor were any of us, German or not. In a way we were in the same boat. They understood this, and I let them know that I felt the same about it.

The best we could do for them was to share our food. We got more of it than we boys needed, and we passed it to them. Later, when we Reisholz *Flakhelfer* were transferred to another site and another battery (in January, see below), I remembered our three Russians more vividly and with more sympathy than the insensitive, heavy-set German loader, the K 3 of the Bertha gun. I often wondered what happened to our Russian friends, whether they perished in the scalding cauldron of war or, despite everything, lived to see their homes again.

Christmas Furlough. On Monday, December 13, winter came to us at last, first with wet snow, then frost, then with a whirling, wind-driven curtain of large flakes that slowly built up on surfaces. The guns were covered with tarps, and the Russians kept shoveling the revetment floor clean. During the following two weeks, the call to man the guns came only three times. The bad weather seemed to hamper the RAF campaign. Still, they hit Berlin during the nights of December 16-17 and 23-24, and Frankfurt, December 20-21. We were on stand-by but the bombers flew in and out around us. We sat tightly squeezed on benches in the narrow bunker, wrapped in overcoats. A wood fire burned in a little metal stove in one corner, its surfaces and the pipe penetrating through the roof gave us some warmth. Next to and across from the stove sat Tylia and the loader, then us *Flakhelfer* and our Russians toward the door. We mostly sat in silence. Only Tylia and the loader made small talk occasionally. We seemed immersed in our own thoughts.

I wondered if the Russians might be thinking of times of snow and cold in their country. Did they recall the happiness of being with their families in the warmth of their homes when outside the wind shrieked across a world that seemed to have turned to ice? Especially, I wondered about Vassiliy from Lake Baikal. Could he tell me what winter was like in Siberia and how he used to cope with it? I remembered snow time from years ago, when we sledded until we were stiff with cold. I went home and my mother prepared a hot salt bath for my feet and a cup of steaming hot chocolate I could barely hold in my hands. Or Bad Einsiedel winter days. Pine forests bending under the weight of snow. The quiet, peaceful, untainted white world, with its pure air and red deer hoof prints in secretive and mysterious designs. But here, I sat in a dark hollow of a bunker sparsely lit from the fire that flickered through the half open hatch of the stove. Wasted time, hours of nothingness, snippets of memory of happier times.

The good news for me was that Tylia let me go on Christmas furlough on the weekend of December 25 to 26. It was fortunate that Christmas Day that year 1943, fell on a Saturday. Werner from our gun crew got to go, too. We were replaced, as always, by the extra boys beyond the required number of three *Flakhelfer* per gun, boys kept for the purpose of taking over gun positions for those on furlough.

Ah, Christmas, my mother's favorite time. The Christ Child coming, the day glowed like a light in the darkness of winter's snow and icy rain. For weeks she had been baking cookies, *Zimtsterne*, *Spekulatius*, *Honigkuchen*, *Spitzkuchen*. Preparinq the *Stollen*, the traditional Christmas cake, was not baking. It was a ritual, a cult come alive. She handled the ingredients with utmost care, measuring and kneading, with an attention usually reserved for the sacred. Before the *Stollen* was placed in the oven the heat was brought to the precise desired degree. Then the waiting began. When the time came for a quick check, I am sure silent prayers were said. When the *Stollen* was removed, as carefully as a baby in a Caesarian section, it was inspected anxiously and with awe. Did it have the right color, the proper height, was it firm? If all these requirements were met, there was jubilation.

Our Christmas tree, when I was little, was brought in on Christmas Eve and decorated while I was in bed. The gifts had been placed under the tree and covered. I was awakened early in the morning, but prevented from looking into the living room. We dressed, and, without breakfast, walked in the dark, often snowy or raining night, to St. Margaretha Basilica. Our Christmas Mass celebration took place at 4 A.M. J.S. Bach on the organ, solemn Baroque songs, candles, candles, the large nativity scene set up in the aisle near the altar, the festive atmosphere, the solid crowd of worshippers dressed in their Sunday coats. Every bench was filled, the aisle, too, with people standing. I always stood with my father. The long, never-ending sermon, the organ again and again. With most of the crowd my mother always went for Holy Communion. Sometimes my father and I did too. Finally, near dawn, the mass ended and we walked through the cold streets to our home. The electric candles of the tree were lit while I waited outside the room. My mother rang a little silver bell and I stormed into the room, into the presence of the lights, the beautiful tree with its ornaments, the gifts, into a miracle.

My mother never wanted to part with the tree. She kept it and lit it every evening until the end of Christmas time in February. Before then the branches had sagged and most of the needles were gone. One last evening of light, of gratitude and sadness. Next morning the skeletal tree was stripped of candles and ornaments and lifted through the window into the dead flower garden.

The Christmas tree was up when I arrived at noon that Saturday. It was a fir eight feet high, and a marvel that my parents had gotten it. We admired it together. There was no *Stollen* for Christmas this time because the necessary ingredients were not available. But my mother had been able to bake *Zimtsterne* and *Spekulatius* and a cake with fruit from our garden. My father had purchased another rabbit, but before we could sit down for dinner we went to St. Margaretha for Christmas Mass. It was held in late afternoon instead of the early morning hours because of the danger of an air raid.

The church was nearly filled as in my memory. The organ played J. S. Bach again, the nativity scene was set up. It looked like it had of old but it wasn't the same. The people were haggard, strained, poorly clothed. There were soldiers in the crowd, on furlough, two of them on crutches and one with his arm in a cast. The sermon was brief, the reading of the names of the recently killed in action short but emotional. So many missing, gone or merely somewhere else. The traditional songs were sung strongly, but almost with despair. We didn't say much on the way home. But then the tree was lit and flooded the room with light. It was Christmas after all. We were alive and together. There were no impressive gifts but we had much we were grateful for. It was a beautiful Christmas. Outside the blanket of snow lay silent and pristine, a marvelous contrast to the candle light inside. The sense of peace extended and there was no alarm during those two nights.

January 4 1944. With an east wind the cold lingered but the days and nights were cloudless, clear. Two nights we were called to the guns when the English attacked Berlin, December 29-30, and January 1-2 1944. We spent time in the bunker but the bombers took a route back far from us. New Year's Eve was a sad experience but New Year's Day was no better. We had all had better New Year's in our lives, the two soldiers next to us, we three *Flakhelfer* and our three Russians. There was no reason to celebrate the past year or the new one. We were depressed. There was nothing to look forward to. All we expected was more of the same. Once we were called to stand-by when American *Viermots* hit Ludwigshafen again, on December 30. But we never got to see them.

Our time came on January 4. American aircraft flew in over Zeeland, southern Holland, and aimed straight east. First it was suspected that this might be a diversion and they would change course. But this time they didn't. When the leading formations passed north of Antwerp, sirens throughout the Ruhr and, the Rhineland howled to drive the civilian population into shelters. When the Flak around Mönchen-Gladbach let loose and kept firing without being drowned out by the rumble of carpet bombing we thought we were in for it. Far to the west we saw the sky fill with vapor trails and tiny specks of approaching aircraft. Tylia reported us ready, the windows in front of the K 1, K 2 and K 6 positions came alive. I sat in the K 6 chair, Vassiliy the K 4, stood next to me. He had placed two shells into the cups of the fuse-setting apparatus and held another shell in his arm, cradling it like a baby. One remembers these little details. For a moment our eyes met.

The growing growl of approaching aircraft. Flak to the west of the city started and then our turn came. *Gruppe* after *Gruppe* left the Bertha barrel. Between shots we heard the roar of the *Viermots* almost above us, mixed with other sounds as heavy bombs whistled on the way down. They detonated close by and the earth, even in the walled-in gun emplacement, seemed to shake. And it continued. There were no *Christbäume*, of course. The bombardier of the lead Fortress targeted visually, as did our command post. The bombers flew over the city from west to east, starting the bomb carpet on the city quarters along the Rhine, laying it across the already largely demolished downtown toward the eastern edge. Fifteen minutes and it was over. The Düsseldorf Flak, our battery included, had done as well as could be expected. A couple of Fortresses were brought down, others had been damaged and left their formations. Their fate would probably be sealed by our fighter planes.

Over the city, smoke and dust clouds arose. Someone pointed to the southwest. There we also saw black smoke flags, the results of bombing Neuss, the neighboring city across the river. Both cities had been struck at the same time. The closest the bombs had come to us was two kilometers to the north. We in the battery had been spared again. If the bombers had started their run from the south, we would probably have been in the target zone. We looked on in silence. The vapor trails in the sky slowly disappeared.

A day after the raid a rumor went around that shook us up. It was said that our battery was to be transferred somewhere without *Flakhelfer*. If it were true, that meant the battery would be sent outside the country, perhaps to the coast of France where massive fortifications were being built in preparation for an Allied invasion expected to come in summer or even spring. What about us *Flakhelfer*? We wondered what would happen to us. We were sure that they would not let us go – but where would they send us? I asked Tylia as Ferdi and Thei asked their gun chiefs. They shrugged. They said they didn't know anything yet. But they agreed that there might be something to the rumor.

Before lunch in the mess hall on January 6, all *Flakhelfer* of the battery were gathered. The battery chief told us that *4. Schwere Flakabteilung 177/0* would cease operations on January 17 and be removed after that date. *Flakhelfer* from Hilden *Gymnasium* were to do duty in a 10.5cm battery at Scholven Hydrier Werk, a hydrogenation synthetic oil plant near Gelsenkirchen. *Flakhelfer* from Rethel *Gymnasium* were transferred to Chemische Werke Hüls, a chemical and synthetic rubber plant near Recklinghausen, where they would do duty in a 2cm light flak Battery. Hüls, that was us. So we were all sent into the Ruhr, the most heavily bombed region in all of Germany. Why us? Why shift us from heavy Flak to light Flak? Why not use us close by? Why send the Hilden *Flakhelfer* to Scholven?

No questions were raised. There would be no answers. The military made decisions based on things recommended at higher levels. They might be questionable to us, but we had no say in it.

I was granted a last furlough for the weekend of January 8 to 9 when I could tell my parents. There was an incident before that, on January 7. We were at lunch in the mess hall when we heard a plane approaching, flying low. The door of the mess hall was thrown open and someone barked, "Out! Out!" We ran toward the guns. The plane was above us, perhaps 400 meters high, a Fortress with one smoking engine, two engines dead, holes in hull and fuselage. We stopped and looked. The great bird in its death throws slowly flew on and, less than a kilometer away, was hit by a 2cm *Vierling* (four-barreled gun) section on the Rhine. They tore it apart in the air. Fragments plunged into the river. Someone in that plane had doggedly kept on against all odds. Some courage!

I told my parents about our Hüls assignment over the weekend. I would not be able to see them twice a month. My mother tried not to, but she cried. My father sat with a hard, stony face. I promised to write often and visit as soon as I could. It was a sad weekend. When I left on Monday morning my mother saw me off as if I were going to the frontline.

3

Flakhelfer, Hüls

January 18-September 22 1944

Journey through the Ruhr. For the next nine days, January 10-16, we worked with the *Geschütz-Staffel* personnel and additional Russians to empty the reserve ammo bunkers along the railroad track and loaded shell boxes on lorries. There were only two alarms, a daytime raid by American bombers on Halberstadt, Osnabrück and Braunschweig, January 11, and a night raid by the RAF on Braunschweig once again, January 14-15. For us, both were false alarms. On January 18, before the removal of the battery began, we *Flakhelfer* from Rethel *Gymnasium* were loaded with our gear on two trucks and started on the road north. We were 31 boys who had served in the *Mess-Staffel* and *Geschütz-Staffel*.

The night before, on the last day of the Reisholz battery's readiness for action, we said good-bye to the men we had been with for months. Together, we spent many hard nights and easy nights, endless hours of waiting for what eventually came, or didn't, lonely nights when nothing could be done but leave one to one's thoughts. Tylia patted me on the shoulder. He came close to embracing Paulchen but didn't. Perhaps he thought soldiers didn't do that. He was quite emotional, though, and wished me well. I did the same. When I left I climbed the revetment wall and looked at Bertha for a last time. We had spent many nights with her. The gun was the one solid presence we held on to as all around us inferno threatened. Working the instruments kept us from giving in to our fear.

My good-bye to the Russians was emotional. Ilya, Piotr, even reserved Vassiliy who kept so much locked up within himself, kissed me on both cheeks the Russian way to say farewell.

On Monday, January 17, our loyal teachers, Pedi and Wallerich, arrived as expected. We had had no chance to tell them earlier that we were being sent elsewhere. We told them then. They were not relieved that their commitment had ended. They were disheartened, saddened. They had tried hard to make us learn under terrible circumstances. They knew that we would need it one day, if we survived. When they were gone I became aware that another phase of my life had ended.

At battery headquarters we got our papers to pass on to the battery in Hüls. In those papers it was duly recorded that we of the Bad Einsiedel contingent had been participants in the destruction of sixteen aircraft, mostly English, with which the Reisholz battery had been credited for the period of June 11 1943, to January 17 1944. How this record was established remained a mystery to me, since we were not the only battery shooting at the invaders. An evaluation by higher command. Perhaps they knew something we didn't. We did not question the results, but I must say we were not impressed. We knew that we had missed a lot more often than we actually hit a target.

The journey took us into the Ruhr area. The trucks avoided our wrecked city and skirted its eastern fringe by going up into the hill country of the Bergische Land to Mettmann. From there, we followed narrow roads through small, still largely intact towns like Velbert, toward Essen. In Hattingen on the Ruhr River, on the edge of Essen, we entered an apocalyptic landscape. We knew what Düsseldorf was like after so many raids, but Essen looked worse. We passed through ruins, countless charred skeletons of façades, remnants of factories and steel mills, devastated neighborhoods. The trucks went on to Bochum and the nightmare continued. The English had waged the "First Battle of the Ruhr" in spring and summer of 1943, leveling the major industrial centers of western Germany. From Reisholz we did our part to stop it but had little success. We had seen the Ruhr cities burn from a distance. Now we saw the extent of destruction from up close. We sat in silence as the trucks rumbled on. Past Bochum we let Gelsenkirchen lie to the west. Even from a distance we recognized that the city was in a similar condition to the ones we had seen. Twelve kilometers farther to the northeast, we got to Recklinghausen. It lay largely buried in rubble like the others.

The sergeant who drove the first truck asked a passer-by for direction. The trucks turned north. Beyond the city we went by patches of forest, a coal mine, and the Hüls Chemical Factory, which was so well camouflaged that we didn't see it. Eventually, standing by a road in front of a birch forest, we reached our destination, battery headquarters, a group of wooden barracks. We were expected. Our journey over a distance of a mere 50 kilometers as the raven flies, had taken us four hours.

Hüls, 4th Battery, *Leichte Flakabteilung 881*. We climbed out of the trucks and stretched. A sergeant-major emerged from one of the barracks, battery headquarters as we learned, and received the report of the sergeant who had led our trucks. They exchanged a quick salute. He called us *Flakhelfer* to form up in ranks and wait. The battery chief stepped from headquarters and stood in front of us.

We looked him over. He was an *Oberleutnant*, medium-sized, with an open face. No iron cross on his chest but a medal we didn't recognize. He was a homeland Flak officer and had not been decorated for combat service. We wondered. Our two Reisholz officers, a Captain and a First Lieutenant, had both worn Iron Crosses first class for performance in action. He looked us over, too. He must have noticed that all of us wore the *Flakkampfabzeichen* we had earned in Reisholz on our dress uniforms. He greeted us and made us welcome.

He explained that the battery consisted of four *Züge* (sections) spread along five kilometers at the northeastern edge of the Chemische Werke Hüls from the Rhein-Herne Kanal in the north to Zeche (coal mine) Ewald in the south. South of us and to the west three more batteries of light Flak with 2cm and 3.7cm guns formed a ring around the factory. Farther out was a second ring of Flak defenses, batteries of heavy guns of 8.8cm, 10.5cm and 12.8cm calibers. The light batteries were charged with protecting against low-level air attacks. The planes we had to be concerned about were American fighters like P-38 Lightnings, P-51 Mustangs and P-47 Thunderbolts. These had recently begun to fly daytime long range bomber escort into Germany. Low-level attacks on Hüls by American fighters should be expected.

He paused. He didn't seem to like what he was telling us. He informed us we were the new gun crews of the battery. His original gun crews had been transferred. He said he regarded us as experienced young soldiers and expected us to adapt quickly to the 2cm weapons. Assignments to the four sections would be handled by the sergeant-major. He looked at our faces, thoughtfully, perhaps with regret, even sorrow, saluted and dismissed us.

The sergeant-major took our papers and divided us up among the sections. Six of us were ordered to *1. Zug*, located in the birch forest north of headquarters. Another six to *2. Zug*, on the south wall of the canal farther north. Five went to *4. Zug* in the south, across from the entrance to coal mine Ewald. Fourteen to *5. Zug*, the *Vierling* section, located in an open field southeast of headquarters. Five of us of the Reisholz shack were able to stay together, sent to *4. Zug*: Ferdi, Thei, Wenner, Hannes and I. Bergittimus, our sixth buddy, was allotted to the *Vierling* section.

While formalities were cleared and paperwork finished, the section chiefs were called in by radio and arrived to take charge of us. Ours was a slender, friendly man in his late 30s. He introduced himself to us as Corporal Sieber and learned our names. From his way of speaking, using sharp s-sounds, we thought he was from the Hamburg area. We gathered our gear and followed him to *4. Zug.* We crossed the east-west trending hard-top road and walked on a foot trail south among birches and blackberry bushes. To the east lay an open field. In the middle, on the west side, stood three barracks and four sod-covered revetments. From three of them rose the barrels of *Vierling* guns. This was *5. Zug.*

As we walked the Corporal told us that the Hüls plant had been bombed severely once. It had been a daytime raid by American Fortresses on June 22 1943. No major attack had occurred since but one could come at any time. That was not good news. We would be sitting ducks in our 2cm gun stations with no chance to fight back as we had in Reisholz. He pointed out steel canisters spaced throughout the area. *Nebeltonnen* (smoke canisters), containers with a poisonous liquid that discharged a dense fog when ignited from a central command. These canisters were activated on days when enemy formations approached the Ruhr. Any such approach could have Hüls as the target. The whole huge factory complex was concealed by layers of camouflage nets. The first indication of enemy aircraft flying in would be the gushing of fog from the canisters, well before an anti-aircraft alarm was sounded. The chemicals in the fog caused a burning sensation in eyes and respiratory systems. Breathing was difficult in this fog. What the unavoidable inhalation of this chemical soup would do to us in the long run nobody knew. Nothing good, we thought.

One and a half kilometers south of headquarters we entered pine forest and came to a wooden tower with three floors above a ground-level storage bin. The corporal's quarters were on the second floor, ours on the third. The fourth was the gun platform. The tower sat twenty meters east of a hard-top road that led from Recklinghausen past Zeche Ewald and the Hüls plant to the east-west road and headquarters. The gate of Ewald was straight across from us. We climbed the winding stairs that led up and around the tower and took our gear to the third floor. Behind the door were a nice living room and separated sleeping quarters with three bunk beds with two cots. We had three windows. One faced the street, the others south and north.

After we put our gear away the corporal took us upstairs and removed the tarp from the body of the single barrel 2cm cannon. We were curious about the gun. We had never seen one before. He explained positions: K 1, the gun layer on a seat behind and to the right of the barrel; K 2, ammunition gunner, sitting on the left side of the gun, charged with feeding magazines into the breech; K 3, ammunition gunner, to supply the K 2 with magazines from a small bunker in the wooden side wall of the platform. He asked who wanted to be K 1. I volunteered. He accepted and explained that the other positions would be switched among us.

Because only three of us were needed to serve the gun, we wondered what the other two would do. He said the battery expected to get one more gun to this section. There were two more Flak towers of *4. Zug* behind us, currently empty. When the gun came, he would request one more *Flakhelfer* from headquarters. Both 1. and *2. Zug* had two guns each; only *4. Zug* had just one. He smiled and shook his head. It didn't matter to him that we were not fully equipped. It didn't bother us either.

The tower had been built high enough so that the gun platform was well above the tops of the surrounding trees. We stood by the rampart and looked around. We had a clear field of fire to the southwest, west and northwest. The corporal pointed out where the factory stood hidden under its thick coat of camouflage. He told us that Hüls was considered the worst poison mill in the German chemical arsenal. Rumors had it that terrible, top secret concoctions were produced there. We had no reason not to believe him. Stationed on a high wooden tower, close to what had to be considered a prime target by English and American bomber commands, left us with a queasy feeling. He tried to dismiss our concerns. During an alarm, when high level attacks were expected, we were allowed to clear the tower and seek shelter below. Where? Was there a bomb shelter? No, he said, we had to take cover in foxholes. Had he done that we asked. Yes, he admitted, a few times.

We wondered what we had gotten into.

4. Zug. We learned quickly about the difference between a heavy Flak battery and a light one like the one we were in now. Where the heavies each had their own fire control command post with radar installations and optical equipment for visual ranging, our battery of 2cm guns had neither. We would receive instructions from a central command that alerted us to incoming and outgoing enemy formations and their operational heights. At night we would be blind. We could only shoot at what we could see. In daytime, enemy aircraft had to come into our limited range before we could go into action. Bombers, day and night, could only be reached by the heavies. We would be spectators to the drama that played out high above us. Although enemy fighters had been spotted in combat with German fighters, none had yet come low enough for the Hüls light cannon. Night alarms could mean that our factory was a target and we should get ready to visit our foxholes.

It took us only a short time to familiarize ourselves with the 2cm gun. I whirled the gun around, played with raising and lowering the barrel, and explored the sighting system. It was quite different from a rifle's but could be managed. Work on the 8.8cm in Reisholz had been heavy duty. This was child's play in comparison.

On that first day we had missed lunch, taken in the mess hall at battery headquarters at 1200 hours every day. Breakfast and supper were delivered to us and our corporal from the kitchen by a Russian *Hiwi*. When he arrived that first evening we learned his first name was Sasha, and that he had been a mathematics teacher in a school at home. That was fortunate. We thought we might call on his expertise some time.

We inspected the foxholes before we took to our cots. There was a brief alarm during the night. We stood on the gun platform around the corporal who wore earphones and a microphone, then retired to our quarters after the English bombers had flown on to Berlin.

On the following morning we worked with the gun, satisfying our corporal. He was very laid-back, not a demanding person. He spent all his time in his room by the radio. We didn't know what he listened to and didn't care. We imagined that he listened to the BBC broadcasts but never asked him about it. Listening to the BBC was considered a serious offense by military authorities and could be severely punished. Our corporal turned out to be a good and decent man. He seemed to feel very lonely. Once he mentioned in passing that something serious had happened to his family in Hamburg, but did not explain. He kept it to himself, and we didn't pry.

Before lunch we had surveyed what there was of *4. Zug*: two empty Flak towers, two wooden barracks with equipment, two ammunition bunkers dug into the ground and covered with sod, and our foxholes. We had walked through our patch of pine forest to the open field and gazed across to *5. Zug*, the biggest of our outfits. This was our world now.

Leisure Time. During this first week a pattern was set that was maintained for the whole time we were in *4. Zug* and that was for most of our time in Hüls. In the mornings, after we took breakfast in our living room, and the corporal took it in his, we all met on the gun platform. We talked a little while about aircraft, theirs and ours, different types of fighter planes, their speed and armament. Sometimes we went through an exercise with the gun. But there was only so much to know, and we had learned it already. We split off quickly. The corporal went to his radio room and left us to our devices. Of course, we had to hang around the tower within the sound radius of the alarm bell. Sometimes we played soccer a stone's throw away. Most of the time, in good weather, we stayed on the platform and read. I was able to read a lot. I finished all the books my mother got

Gunner's tower, *4. Zug*, Hüls, spring 1944.

At the foot of *4. Zug* gun tower. Author in middle, Ferdi to his right, Wenner to his left. Hüls, March 1944.

Playing with a French machine-gun on *4. Zug* gun platform. Wenner is in foreground, Thei in middle, Hannes in background. Hüls, summer 1944.

Author on the gunner's seat. *4. Zug*, Hüls, spring 1944.

me from the old public library unter den Eichen. At nights, when the English flew by, we gathered on the platform, connected to a source of information through the corporal's earphones. Once the bombers passed, we went back to our rooms. During a daytime alarm, we removed the tarp from the sleek 2cm and waited. Nothing came our way. Sometimes, at night, there was a brief alarm when an English Mosquito came over and dropped a single bomb on or near the factory, perhaps to remind us we were not forgotten. On such occasions we crouched in our foxholes, listening to the angry Flak fire of the heavies and, sometimes, hearing the awful whistling sound of a bomb coming down. I was relieved when I heard it. The saying was, "if you hear it, it's gone somewhere else, if you don't, it hits you."

At the first lunch after our arrival, we were fitted at headquarters with wooden clogs. We were expected to wear them in the sections and around the guns. We never figured out why. Was it to save shoe leather or had someone higher up made a special deal with a Dutch manufacturer? The clogs were cumbersome. We got used to them but never liked them. They made us slow and ponderous. Only on our midday trips to the mess hall could we wear shoes.

The English attacked Berlin four times and Magdeburg once during our first three weeks, but passed the Ruhr by. American bombers were more active than the English at that time. They attacked Magdeburg and Halberstadt on January 27, Eschweiler on the 24th, Frankfurt on the 29th, Braunschweig and Hannover on the 30th, Frankfurt again on February 4, 8, and 11, and Braunschweig once more on the 10th. All these attacks were far away from us. Three times we saw vapor trails of American bomber boxes and twice we watched dog fights between Focke Wulf fighters and, we thought, Mustangs. They drew wild swirls and pirouettes across the sky, playing a deadly game before our eyes. Although we saw no victims and no victors, somewhere someone scored and someone died.

My mother wrote me regularly; usually my father added a note. They tried to be positive but between the lines I understood their worry, and not for me alone. I knew what they thought, how despairing they had become. I wrote to them, too, telling them that I was safe. Compared to Reisholz, I told them, Hüls was like a vacation. We hardly had any duties and got much time for ourselves. Our gun chief was a fine man who, remarkably, imposed little on us.

This was all true so long as one ignored the constant fear of a massive air attack on the factory. I didn't mention that. We lived in pleasant isolation. We only saw the battery chief and the sergeant-major occasionally in the mess hall at lunch; none of them ever came for an inspection or even a visit. The only persons we were in constant contact with were the corporal and Sasha, our kitchen man. He waited while we had breakfast and supper, and when he left, we let him take the rest of the supplies home, including what we didn't want. This, especially, was the sweet milk-noodle soup we had already encountered in Reisholz. It was exclusively served to *Flakhelfer*. Someone higher up must have thought we needed it since we were still growing up and all. But we despised the soup; Sasha and his fellow Russians seemed to love it.

Despite bad things happening around us everywhere, we in *4. Zug*, although bored sometimes, felt pretty good about ourselves and where we were. It could have been much worse.

A bit of change that didn't alter our general situation came on February 14, a Monday. All *Flakhelfer* of the battery met in the largest barrack available, the one of the gun crews of *5. Zug*. Finally, a *gymnasium* teacher had been found who would teach classes for three hours on Monday and Tuesday mornings. He was a man in his fifties who had to travel to us by railroad from Dortmund, 30 kilometers away. Sometimes he could not reach Recklinghausen because of an air alarm. And sometimes we had to rush from class to our respective sections when our alarm bell tolled. Under these conditions, school was pretty haphazard.

His teaching credentials were in math and chemistry, and these two fields he tried to convey to us. He was nothing like Wallerich, our math teacher in Reisholz, a man with a good heart and understanding from whom we had learned quite a bit despite the frequent alarms. This new teacher was an authoritarian, a hard man, a stickler for protocol. This was something we were not used to, even in our military experience. We were not cadets in a Nazi Party educational establishment. We saw ourselves as young soldiers who had already proven themselves. He must have felt our resentment, our growing hostility. He tried to break it down with even stiffer control. I didn't work. We ignored him. He threatened not to pass us to the next higher grade, *Untersekunda* in *gymnasium* grade rankings. We heard this threat, but when the time came for this decision, some of us talked with our battery chief. He had a few words with the teacher and we were passed. I learned a bit more math during that time, but nothing in chemistry.

Furlough. I got my first furlough in Hüls for the weekend of February 19-20. Early On Saturday morning I walked to the edge of Recklinghausen where I took a streetcar to the railroad station. The city looked like others in the Ruhr and Rhineland. Over half the buildings and apartment complexes were destroyed. Most of the station lay in ruin, but the railroad track had been repaired. It was a wonder that the railroad system still functioned despite the savage destruction wrought by the bombings. The train south took me through Herne, Bochum, Essen, and Mülheim; each had been attacked many times. Now I saw the apocalyptic setting the Ruhr district had become from a train window. The view was worse than from our trucks. Because the railroad line went through the hearts of the cities, and the hearts of all these cities had been among the chief targets, the train passed through one scene of desolation after another. Arriving in the Düsseldorf main station was no reprieve from what I had seen passing through the others. After all, during my seven months in Reisholz our city had suffered severe attacks five times, on June 11-12 and 25-26, August 22-23, November 2-3 1943, and on January 4 1944. I had been there and recorded what happened in my diary.

I arrived at my parents' house in early afternoon. It had rained earlier. The streets were wet under a leaden sky. The great trees in front of the house, bereft of their foliage, looked dead with beds of dead leaves under them. The dark colors of winter lay everywhere, as dark as the stone masonry of our house, dark as the shale shingles that covered the steep roof. After the gloomy train journey through the desolation of the Ruhr cities, and the disheartening streetcar ride through the equally drab ruins of my home city, I had the overwhelming sensation that everything was dead or dying. I approached the heavy iron door of the entrance with its reddish patination and rang the bell. I knew that my parents expected me; I had written to tell them I would come.

But then there was my mother, embracing me, laughing, but close to tears, my father's somber face lightened by a big smile. I was surprised at the magnitude of their happiness at having me back. I was still dejected by what I had seen on the way home and by my gloomy thoughts. If they recognized my mood, they ignored it. They seemed determined to create as much joy from our reunion as possible. At first I shrank back, freezing up, but then, slowly, I yielded. Their happiness was contagious. My mother talked mostly about little things, old nice things we enjoyed remembering. Slowly, I began to feel comfortable. Spending day and night with my buddies, sharing danger and boredom, food and thought, experiences, everything, it set us apart from civilians, even from the people who should be closest to a sixteen year old, his parents.

There were lines in my parents' faces I had not noticed before. We stayed on subjects that were pleasant and not offensive. We didn't talk about the war. We didn't have to. I knew my parents regarded the war as lost and were afraid that the Nazis would fight on with us as pawns until, as the marching song every *Jungvolk*-Hitler Youth boy learned said, "Wir werden weitermarschieren, bis alles in Scherben faellt… " ("We'll go on marching till all lies in shambles ... "). I mentioned the good things about Hüls and omitted others. Dinner in the evening was good, pork chops. My parents had saved meat allowed on their ration cards for this event. The table was set carefully as always, crystal, fine china, silverware. There were reasons to be thankful.

These became two good days after all. Air raid alarms sounded both nights and we spent time in the basement shelter. But the English had flown on elsewhere. The radio in the morning said that Leipzig and Stuttgart had been attacked. On a rainy morning I took the dismal journey back feeling better than when I'd come.

A Nightfighter's Night. Returning, walking away from the Recklinghausen end station of the streetcar line, I could see and smell the acid-tasting fog while I was still two kilometers from the *4. Zug* tower. Before I got there, air raid sirens howled. I rushed up the stairs, dropped my gear and book satchel in our apartment and hastened to the gun platform. They were all there, standing around the corporal with serious expressions on their faces. "Amis over Rotterdam," Ferdi whispered to me. Sieber listened intently to a new message coming through the earphones. He looked at the floor. "They are over Emmerich now, continuing east." Emmerich was 75 kilometers northwest of us. Considering that a Fortress was supposed to have a maximum speed of 475 km/h, somewhat less fully loaded, the bombers could reach us in fifteen minutes or less if Hüls was the target. Getting down from the tower and into the foxholes would take five minutes, so we had less than ten minutes to spare, waiting for more news. The heavy Flak to the north had not opened up. Perhaps they might pass us by?

The bomber fleet did pass. They hit Braunschweig, 250 kilometers east-northeast of us. There were American fighter planes with the *Viermots*, Lightnings and Mustangs. What would they do if their escort was not needed? We remained on the tower for three hours until the last of the armada left the air space north of us on their way back.

There was no school in the morning. And there was none on the following morning. That day was a repetition of Monday. Again we wasted hours on the tower while the bomber stream passed us to the north and hit Magdeburg, 75 kilometers east of Braunschweig. On the way back it came into the range of the heavies on the edge of the Ruhr around Dorsten, Marl and those in the north of Recklinghausen. We watched the build-up of vapor trails from a safe distance.

Relentless day and night attacks continued. On the 24th the Americans bombed Schweinfurt again and the English followed with an attack during the night. As in their earlier raids on the Schweinfurt ball-bearing industry, the Fortresses and Liberators suffered grievous losses. During the night we watched an interesting spectacle from our tower. In a cloudless sky English Lancasters and Halifaxes flew in a steady stream relatively low, about 5,000 meters (16,000 feet) high. Each plane was separated from the next by a kilometer or more. The searchlights had a great night. They picked them up one after another. As each rode the light cone, heavy Flak set to work on it, until passing it on to the next string of batteries. The shooting was pretty accurate due to visual ranging.

One plane was brought down. Six times the Flak ceased firing when sudden flares were dropped behind a Viermot. Shortly thereafter, we saw tracers and the *Viermot* burst into flames and came down. Six *Abschüsse* by nightfighters. This was a bad night for the RAF. We saw something like this only once more during our time in Hüls. It was obvious we knew little about what hard battles were fought in the sky.

We had school again in *5. Zug* on Monday but the next day, February 29, Americans hit Braunschweig again and we spent another three hours on the tower. Until my next furlough, March 18-19, we had class just four times, March 6 and 7, and March 13 and 14. Math and chemistry got the short end of the stick compared to our other chores. Most days we spent hours and hours on the tower on stand-by as the Americans flew no less than seventeen raids on major cities beyond the Ruhr, including two in our old neighborhood, Köln and Bonn, March 4. And so our lives went.

My weekend furlough was similar to the last one. My parents and I were happy to be together. On Sunday afternoon I took the .22 to the *Ruine*. My hunting ground looked forlorn, its magic lost. I walked in the wet grass and once sat for a while on a pile of stones that had fallen from the crest of the castle keep. Everything was fading away, nothing remained as it had been. I left in the morning with another load of books, German classical and post-classical literature – the best company for a wounded heart.

A Promotion. During the following four weeks we had classes Monday and Tuesday mornings; for a change they were not interrupted by alarms. The fog canisters remained a threatening presence during class sessions, but did not get into action. Nevertheless, American bombers flew nine missions into Germany while we sat useless on our tower during six of them. The teacher from Dortmund dropped chemistry and focused on math. We agreed that we needed math most; teaching chemistry without a lab was impossible. The going was so tough that we called on Sasha, our Russian math teacher, to help us with homework and prepare us for in-class exams. With his help we managed. I had been never fond of math, so I barely got by.

A couple of events occurred during that time that stood out and disrupted our routine. One day we were all promoted to *LW-Oberhelfer*, the highest grade available, our promotions because of seniority. From then on we wore a thin silver cord on both shoulder straps of our dress uniform. We also received the *Flakleistungsabzeichen*: (Flak Merit Badge). This was an oval piece of blue-grey cloth 10cm (3¾ inches) wide, embroidered with silver yarn depicting an 8.8cm cannon between eagle wings with oak leaves attached and a small swastika underneath. This piece had to be sewn on to the lower left sleeve of the dress uniform. I recorded neither the promotion to *Oberhelfer* nor the decoration in my diary, so I have no dates for them. We proudly wore the silver cords on our dress uniforms because they signified that we were *alte Hasen* ("old hares") who had been under fire. We were ambivalent about the merit badge. In Reisholz we had fought to protect our cities and others. We did nothing in Hüls that deserved praise.

Another event was the repetition of what had happened on February 24-25. The English once again bombed Schweinfurt, March 30-31, and again on a clear night. On the way back, the Lancasters and Halifaxes followed the same route that had brought them such harm five weeks earlier. Searchlights picked them up and passed them from one battery to the next. We saw four *Viermots* shot down by Flak and one by night- fighter.

Two sad events happened on the nights of March 26-27 and April 11-12. The first was a heavy raid on Essen, once again, the second, a raid on Aachen. Essen was just twenty kilometers south of us. When the bombers approached the Ruhr we thought it might be our turn, the one we anticipated with dread. A short time after the alarm sounded we were ordered to clear the tower. I sat hunched in my foxhole, my head with the steel helmet pressed against the earth, listening to the sounds that came through the night. The rumble of Flak fire accompanied the English bombers from the moment they neared Bottrop and held on from Oberhausen to Essen. So they went elsewhere! Then came the awful sounds of booming explosions, again and again. I climbed out of the foxhole and, with the others, ran up the stairs to the platform. We stood together, leaning against the parapet, and watched pillars of fire and smoke spring up and reach in to the sky and redden the clouds. We had seen it so many times before, but the destruction of a city still caused a shock that burned into our hearts.

We only saw the red sky from the Aachen raid a hundred kilometers to the southwest. The ancient city of Charlemagne, founded at the end of the 8th century A.D., put to the torch, too! When Thei and I went through Essen on furlough on the weekend of April 15-16, we saw the ghastly new scars that had been added three weeks ago atop the old ones from earlier attacks.

Oh Düsseldorf. When the two of us returned on Monday morning, our three buddies were waiting anxiously. We had received orders to transfer to *1. Zug* for the next fourteen days. Someone at battery headquarters had worked out a plan to shuffle gun-crews among the various sections. The section chiefs remained where they were, so our pleasant Corporal Sieber would not go with us. We never learned the reasons for this new system. Perhaps it was thought we had become too complacent or too comfortable in our present haunts.

That was bad news for us. The section chief of *1. Zug*, a sergeant by the name of Kulick, had the reputation of being a boor, a plebeian, and a sexual fiend, according to the *Flakhelfer* who had served under him. They had been very unhappy in *1. Zug*.

We packed our gear and moved out. *1. Zug* was located in the birch forest about 1 kilometer northwest of battery headquarters. There were three wooden towers but only two 2cm guns. The birches were young trees no higher than ten meters (30 feet). The towers, accordingly, had a supply shed on ground level and the gun platforms on the second floor, above the treetops. The buildings of the Hüls factory lay to the south and southwest. We immediately missed our *4. Zug* apartment on the third floor. Now we were quartered in a sizable wooden shack on the ground next to a washroom, about 50 meters from the sergeant's hut. The sergeant made us stand at attention when he explained the situation. He was a burly man in his early forties with a roundish face and no medals on his chest. He eyed us with suspicion; boys from an elite school like the others who thought they were better than him. Or so he had told our predecessors. It didn't matter that we didn't think that way; he lived by his misconceptions and acted upon them.

We were split into two crews to serve the guns. Thei and Wenner stayed with me. Ferdi took the second gun with Hannes. We were forced to do training exercises with the guns. Wasted time. We were already experts at dry runs. We never fired a round while in *1. Zug*. I had test fired short bursts in *4. Zug* a couple of times at night. It was called *Funktions-Schiessen*. At an exact moment all the guns of the battery let loose. The command to fire was given to the section chiefs by radio. I had never shot at, nor even seen, a real target.

There was no class that morning. None on the following day when American *Viermots* came through and bombed Brandenburg, Wittenberge and Oranienburg. Again, we sat for hours on the platforms.

The sergeant never visited the guns during an alarm. He stayed in his hut by the radio and only pushed the alarm button and gave the all-clear signal. He was rarely alone there. Almost every day he was visited by one woman or another. Usually the visitor stayed over night. We could clearly hear them as they carried on. They knew we heard, but they didn't care. Our *Flakhelfer* buddies were right: Kulick was a plebeian and an unabashed sex fiend, as were his women. In the mornings, after the woman had left without giving us a glance, the sergeant tore through our abode playing non- commissioned officer. He made sure our bed covers were straightened to perfection and our lockers were organized according to his demands. The slightest actual or imagined deviation resulted in the "offender" being sent to polish the two-seat latrine. He enjoyed sneering at the books on our table, books for school and books for private reading, before he retired to his hut. Sometimes he left the section without explanation, charging us to cover for him at the radio, and depending on us for keeping quiet about his absence.

On the third night after our arrival in *1. Zug*, April 20-21, Köln was bombed again, and on the night following, Düsseldorf. Twice we watched the burning sky to the west-southwest. The far one on the first night we suspected was Köln. The closer one on the second night we thought was our city. In Reisholz we had learned to identify the locations of huge fires and firestorms at night. We feared for our parents, relatives, neighbors, and friends, and all the others. We watched helplessly. In the morning we learned that the Düsseldorf attack had been severe. We were angry at the "terror bombers." We would have understood if the English bombed Hüls, even though we might not have survived it. After all, Hüls was an important chemical facility, perhaps of relevance to the German war effort. Why did the English hit the same cities again and again when the industries there had already been destroyed, and after destruction reorganized somewhere in the countryside?

We asked for furlough to look for our people in Düsseldorf. It was granted to five of our 31 *Flakhelfer*, and they left immediately. Thei was one of them. They were to check on all our families. Those of us remaining at the battery worried for three days. When the guys came back their news was bad, but not too bad. None of our loved ones had died, although four families lost their homes; they had survived in concrete bunkers. They would be quartered somewhere, but did not know where yet. Their sons were given furlough for a couple of days to be with them. None of the bombs had fallen on Gerresheim. My parents were safe. There was another attack on Essen on April 26-27. We spent some time in the foxholes during that night and later watched the fires from the towers. I was finally granted furlough for the weekend of April 29-30. My parents knew from Thei's visit that we in Hüls were all right. They told me that the attack had caused great damage south of the main railroad station of my city. One thousand two hundred and fifty people were counted dead, others still missing, many injured, and another 25,000 had lost their homes.

5. Zug. When I returned to the battery I went straight to *5. Zug* for class. The Dortmund teacher disliked absences due to furlough; they interfered with his plans. Although interruptions by air raid alarms were frequent and unavoidable, he seemed to think furloughs should be avoidable. To us they were a link to our families and a world threatened but still existing. They gave us a brief release from the life and monotony in the battery.

After class and after lunch we walked the two and a half kilometers to *3. Zug* where we had been transferred. When we passed the *1. Zug* towers and Kulick's shack we felt sorry for the boys who had come up with us and replaced us there. *3. Zug* consisted of three revetments sitting in a line on the wall of the Rhein-Herne Canal, a waterway that connected the Ruhr cities with the Ems River and the North Sea coastal city of Emden. Below the canal wall sat the corporal's hut, a larger wooden barrack for us, the gun crews, and the ubiquitous latrine. There were only two 2cm cannons here also, not the full complement of three. The corporal, by the name of Brand, served as section chief and radio man. He was a heavy-set, jovial man, happy to be stationed in what appeared to be a backwater place in the war. Our association with him was good and friendly. And we, too, felt that we were away from everything, including the Hüls factory.

Over the next fourteen days we had class three times. On Monday, May 4, instead of class we sat in our revetments as American *Viermots* came through on the way to Braunschweig and Berlin. Five times we stood by the guns when the Americans bombed Münster, May 7, Saarbrüeken, May 11, Merseburg and Chemnitz, May 12, and Osnabrück and Stralsund, May 13. Aside from this, we had a good time in *3. Zug*, and as always, much time to ourselves. We got permission to call on Sasha, our Russian genius, for math homework.

On May 14 we transferred to *5. Zug*, along with boys from the other sections to raise the numbers to the required fourteen *Flakhelfer*. This was the first time I sat in the gunner's chair on a 2cm *Vierling*, the K 1 position. I had to make a few adjustments. My left foot fired the lower left and upper right barrels, the right foot the lower right and upper left barrels. The sighting mechanism was the same as on the single-barrel gun. The K 2 position, assistant to the gunner, generally recommended in regulations, was considered superfluous and omitted. The K 3 sat on the left side of the gun, the K 4 on the right side. These were the magazine gunners, charged with feeding magazines into the breeches. The ammunition gunners, K 5 and K 6, were Russian *Hiwis*. The section chief, a *Fähnrich* (officer-candidate), was in a small command post in the middle of the triangle formed by the three revetments. The Russian *Hiwis* were permanently stationed in the *Vierlings-Zug*. We had not met them before but got along with them well.

While we were in *5. Zug* the RAF opened a new campaign on the Ruhr cities and the Rhineland. On May 20-21 Düsseldorf was attacked again, on May 21-22, Duisburg, on May 22-23, Dortmund, and Aachen on May 24-25 and 26-27. During these night attacks we just stood in the open and watched the bloody skies. There was no end to it. What bothered us most, of course, was the repeated bombing of Düsseldorf. Our parents had been spared so far. It was a miracle. But for how much longer? This was a bad time for us. On Tuesday, May 23, the morning after his city had been hit, our teacher from Dortmund did not show up. We knew transportation was disrupted; perhaps he had perished.

On Saturday, May 27, I was granted another furlough. Because of the damage to Duisburg I had difficulty getting to Düsseldorf. Trains had been re-routed. I got there in the evening. On the streetcar to Gerresheim I found out that the suburb was still intact. What a relief! What would I do if my parents were dead? I had no one else. My aunt Lisbeth had lost her large house on Kreuz-Strasse, near the Düsseldorf downtown area, a year ago and was a homeless refugee somewhere in the country. My uncle Peter, the Nazi in the family, was with the Rheinmetall arms factory, destroyed in Düsseldorf but now operating somewhere hidden in the country in a secret location. Even if I knew where to find him, I would never stay with him and his wife. The parents of my cousins who had been killed in action were too distant from us, from me. Without my parents, what would I have to live for?

Inside the Factory. On Monday, May 29, the five of us assembled in *4. Zug* after two weeks in *5. Zug*. We had not heard from our teacher. There would have been no class on that and the following morning anyway because American bombers were in the air, hitting cities like Leipzig and Cottbus on the 29th and

Halberstadt, Dessau and Oldenburg on the 30th. We spent senseless hours on the platform. Once we thought we saw Mustangs and Thunderbolts flying bomber escort, but way out of our range. heavy flak did its best on them. We saw no German fighter planes.

A first happened on June 2. All of us *Flakhelfer* in the battery were marched by the sergeant-major to the Hüls factory to test our gas masks. Military guards opened the gate. We stepped into a different world, a world shadowed by the umbrella of layers and layers of camouflage nets that closed off the sky and the outside. It was eerie, unreal yet real. We marched down a street, passing buildings on both sides. Workers walked from place to place with purpose. We had heard that many men of different nationalities were employed in the factory under guards, supervised by German technicians, engineers, and scientists. Some of these were supposedly prisoners of war, others forced laborers from Russia and occupied Western countries.

We saw a group of prisoners under guard marched by. They all wore striped clothes and caps in blue and white and had detached, emotionless, forlorn faces. It suddenly struck me that they had to be concentration camp prisoners, the first I ever saw. Their eyes glanced over us as they passed. Lifeless. What might they think of us in our uniforms? Fanatical Nazi kids? It came as a shock to us, certainly to me. I remembered how Brownshirts and police had arrested men in our neighborhood who were believed to be prominent in the Communist and Social Democratic Parties back when I was six years old in April-May 1933. These men had disappeared without a trace. And I remembered my father telling me that Jewish citizens were gathered up, put on trains and sent away. Was this where they went? To this place and others like it? Had they been sent into slave labor?

The testing of the gas masks was nothing. In a closed room we put the masks on and some sort of gas was blown in. Afterward we went out and removed the masks.

But what I had seen stayed with me. As *Flakhelfer* we were not prisoners like the workers in the factory or our *Hiwis*. We had some freedom, even got furlough to see our families. But in a way, we were also prisoners of the State and its system. We thought we defended our cities. But without the war our cities would not be bombed, would not need defenses. Yes, there was a war going on, many people dying. Who was responsible? My parents knew. I knew. Most of my buddies didn't dare think that way. What could you do when you know what is wrong? The Nazis executed those who openly questioned the government. In the Hüls factory, I had suddenly been confronted with the truth behind the system we were serving, a truth hidden from the outside. We had just wandered in and seen. Now we were expected to erase it from our memory.

During the following weeks there was a lull in air attacks on Germany. The Allies pounded fortifications on the French coast, submarine bases, rail yards, supply centers, airfields, bridges, and other targets deemed important for the German war effort. It was thought that this was in preparation for an Allied invasion. Expected for weeks, it came on June 6. We stood in Sieber's radio room. We listened to the news that the Allies had landed in Normandy. Another phase of the war had begun. We had heard the Nazi propaganda for months. Enormous fortifications had been built to reject the invasion. Elite troops had been assembled near the coast. We were pretty confident the Allies would be thrown back into the sea. We didn't know about the strengths of the American, English and Canadian forces, thousands of ships lying along the coast and blasting the defenses, thousands of *Viermots* walking bomb carpets inland. After a week it became obvious that the invasion was slowly succeeding. In Russia and Italy our troops were retreating. Could this be the beginning of the end?

During these weeks the RAF flew only one attack on the Ruhr. They struck Gelsenkirchen, twelve kilometers south of us, on June 12-13. Perhaps they intended to remind us that we had not been forgotten during the turmoil in Normandy.

Despite all of this, four of us were granted the vacation that each *Flakhelfer* was guaranteed by law. Wenner, Thei, Hannes and I left for Düsseldorf on Saturday, June 24, to see our parents before traveling to vacationland.

Tyrol. On Monday, June 26, the four of us met at the Düsseldorf main station. *Feldpolizei* (military police) checked the papers of every soldier on the platform waiting for the special train. That included us. A sergeant, with the oval metal shield on his chest that identified him as a military policeman, searched our papers and looked us over. He noted our medals and the silver cords on our shoulder straps. He also observed that we wore the full complement of our dress uniform, including the swastika armband on our left arm. We had slipped the armbands on before we entered the station; we didn't want to give the *Feldpolizei* a reason to penalize us. He was satisfied, saluted and moved on. There was quite a crowd at the station, soldiers returning from furlough to go back to their units in Italy and elsewhere, their girls or wives and children, some mothers and fathers. It was a bitter good-bye for them all when the train came into the station. We noticed that a *Vierling* gun was on a flatbed car behind the two locomotives and another at the end of the train. The train came in from the north and was nearly filled with returning soldiers. We climbed aboard and settled in a compartment with four soldiers from Duisburg. They looked at us with disdain. Perhaps they wondered about the swastika armbands, perhaps they saw us as Hitler's young guards. We were able to correct their misconception during the journey south. Two of them were in their early twenties, one in his thirties, one a bit older. Two of the younger ones wore the Iron Cross Second Class and the Infantry Combat Badge, the oldest, the black medal that meant that he had been wounded in combat. They were not talkative. They were thinking of the bombed-out city where they had been, of the combat they were returning to. The farther south the train rolled, the quieter they became. We, in contrast, were in a fine mood, happy to get away from it all and go on vacation in Austria.

The train picked up soldiers in all the major cities, from Köln through Bonn, Koblenz, Mainz, Stuttgart and München. From the train's windows we could not avoid seeing the terrible damage done to these cities and some of the smaller ones we passed through. Eventually we became as quiet as our companions. Was there really an escape from this? Already by Koblenz, all the train's compartments had filled up and men settled with their gear in the aisles. As the train hurried through the night we caught some sleep piled against each other.

We reached our destination, Innsbruck, in the early morning. The city, the old capital of the Tyrol, was undamaged and a wondrous sight to see. A beautiful city! We walked from the station to the center of the city, admired the famous *Goldene Dacherl*, the Golden Roof, the celebrated landmark, and sat on a bench, taking it all in. I don't remember whose idea it had been to go to Tyrol, but it had been the right one. We munched sandwiches we had brought with us and plotted how to proceed. We decided to spend one night in Innsbruck and then move into the Stubai Valley for our vacation. We took a room in one of the best and best-known hotels (!) in the city, the Weisses Kreuz Hotel. After all, we had accumulated money from our *Flakhelfer* pay and been given more from our parents. Transportation to Innsbruck had been paid by the military. We had money to burn. We had a wonderful day and a peaceful night. On the following morning, we took a slow train into the Stubai Valley to the little town of Neustift, 40 kilometers south of Innsbruck.

Neustift sat in a lovely valley below the Stubaier Alpen twenty-five kilometers northwest of Brenner Pass and the Italian border. We found a little hotel with friendly people who treated us as their own. Perhaps they were sorry for us. The war was a distant menace in this green valley nestled in magnificent mountains.

We spent four marvelous days, hiking, climbing, swimming, and without concern for the rest of the world. A vacation from ourselves or, perhaps, to ourselves. This was life as it should be lived. I remember my time in that place as one of the most precious of my teenage years.

Of course, we removed our swastika armbands. They were as unpopular among the locals as they were with us. But when these days ended we experienced a rude surprise as we entered the Innsbruck railroad station for the trip home. We had not bothered to put the armbands back on and caught the attention of a *Feldpolizei* lieutenant. He barked at us, forced us to stand at attention. First he threatened to arrest us. That of course made no sense because we had to be back in the battery in three days. He looked at our medals and changed his mind. He informed us that he would report us to our battery chief for punishment. That didn't scare us, but it put a lousy finish on a grand vacation. When, three days later, after one day with our parents, we stood before our battery chief, he asked, "*Jungens*, what did you do?" We told him. He nodded and made a contemptuous gesture with his hand, dismissing the incident. He was glad to have us back.

Sweet Seventeen. During the next four weeks we returned to the passive role of observers of the continuing air war. We witnessed the emasculation of hydrogenation synthetic oil plants in the Ruhr, the shredding of industries left in the doomed cities, and the wilful destruction of civilian populations there. These targets were attacked dozens of times day and night. We wondered what was left in Hamburg and München, in Leipzig and Stuttgart, in Frankfurt and Kiel, in Berlin and Königsberg, in Düsseldorf and Cologne and Braunschweig, worthy of raid after raid. If the Allies wanted to demonstrate that their unbelievable power made a continuation of the war sheer folly, we would have agreed, but we were not asked and were in no position to act upon it. We felt like sitting ducks in our foxholes in Hüls. We thought Hüls should have been a prime target, but it was spared.

We wondered about that a lot. We were glad no attack had happened yet, but still expected one at any time.

Still, we were shifted every fourteen days from one Zug to another. During these next four weeks, daytime raids hit no less than 21 cities and the RAF contributed six night- time raids. The one that came closest to us was an attack on Wanne-Eickel, twenty kilometers to the south. We sat in our foxholes, thinking this might be us. When we were told that red and green *Christbäume* flared above Wanne-Eickel, we crawled out of hiding and watched what we could see. It seemed this was just another night, a night such as we experienced over and over.

We got our math teacher back for a total of six class meetings. We still needed Sasha's help. One day he brought us two elaborate bird figurines, carved by one of his comrades who had done the work with a simple pocket-knife. It was gesture of thanks for the sweet soup and the bread and artificial honey we gave Sasha from our rations that he shared with the others.

I went on furlough on Saturday, July 29. My 17th birthday was on the 31st, so my parents and I had to celebrate a day earlier, Sunday. In the morning we went to church. My mother thought it was appropriate. I wasn't sure, but saw no reason not to accept my mother's wish. Again there were a couple of soldiers on furlough present. I guess I was one, too. The priest read the names of fallen members of the congregation from the pulpit, "Gefallen für Führer, Volk and Vaterland." The Catholic Church had no trouble calling Hitler "Führer." She was right that the fallen had indeed been sacrificed by and for the "Führer," but not for the Vaterland: The Fatherland was slowly being demolished piece by piece. I didn't see any indication that the Church, the Vatican, tried to intervene to stop the carnage or supply a genuine message of hope. Prayer and sweet incense were not enough to change the mind of the "Führer." My father and I looked at each other. We were thinking the same thoughts, I believed.

Our midday dinner was a feast. My parents had doubled the skimpy meat ration by buying horse meat instead of beef or pork. My mother had made delicious Sauerbraten (marinated roast in sweet and sour sauce), and my father even produced a bottle of white wine. Before we sat down to eat I was given a little parcel for my birthday. I unwrapped it eagerly. It was a book I didn't know of, Franz Werfel's *Die Vierzig Tage des Musa Dagh* ("The Forty Days of Musa Dagh"). It was a novel about the dramatic resistance of a small Armenian community during the massacres of Armenians in Turkey in 1916.

I was very surprised. How had they gotten it? The government had put Werfel and his books on the list of forbidden literature and, with many other authors and their works, prohibited bookstores and libraries from having copies. My mother had talked with our old librarian friend at the Unter den Eichen Stadtbibliothek. She had removed Werfel and other outlawed authors from the shelves as had been demanded, but she had not destroyed them. Instead, she kept them for the future, she said. She had given the Werfel from her treasures for my birthday. The book was a 1st edition, published by Paul Zsolnay Verlag in 1933.

We didn't talk much about the war. My parents, of course, wanted it to end. If not, I would probably be sucked into the maelstrom. They were always afraid for my life. They knew my days in Hüls were numbered. Soon I would go to the *RAD* (*Reichsarbeitsdienst* – Reich Labor Service) for few months, and from there into the *Heer*.

Still, it was a memorable birthday crowned by two days and nights without air raid alarms.

Ferdi Leaves. On the early afternoon of Tuesday, August 1, Ferdi's father suddenly arrived at our *4. Zug* tower and came up the stairs. It quite surprised us. He brought his son's enlistment order for the *RAD*. We were stunned. We had not expected this to begin so soon. Because he lived next door to my parents, Ferdi's father had asked my mother before leaving for Hüls if a letter from the *RAD* had come for me, too. It hadn't. Now Ferdi had to go to battery headquarters, show the enlistment order, and get his required discharge papers. He also had to deposit his *Flakhelfer* gear there, being a civilian again, at least for a few days. He changed into his civilian clothes and we went with him to turn his stuff in. Each item was counted and duly registered. After the discharge papers were signed and stamped, he was free to leave. We walked with him to *4. Zug* for the last time. After we said good-bye, and watched him and his father walk away on the road to Recklinghausen, we had the feeling of real loss. Our close-nit group of five that had been together for years and had weathered so many bad nights and days, had been cut to four. Which of us would be next, and when?

Two days later our gun was removed, as were one gun each from *1. Zug* and *3. Zug*. It seemed they were more urgently needed elsewhere. Thus the already reduced firepower of the 4th Battery, *Leichte Flakabteilung 881*, was further diminished. *1. Zug* and *3. Zug* retained one 2cm gun each. As before, only *5. Zug* kept the full complement of three *Vierlings*. We of *4. Zug* had a French machine-gun captured in the early phase of the war set up on our tower. It made a poor replacement for the fine gun we lost. We wondered what this all meant. Were we expected to try to repel an Allied low-level attack with a puny machine-gun like this? We thought it was time for all of us to move on.

The news from Normandy was terrible. On August 12 an American offensive broke through the western sector of the German front and our troops were in retreat. On August 19, US forces had reached the Seine River and by August 25, Paris was taken. Often we stood around Sieber's radio and listened with him. We didn't understand the sudden collapse. The Allies had not made major gains for over two months. But we knew what it meant. If they couldn't be stopped in Normandy, they couldn't be stopped anywhere.

Despite what was going on during these weeks in France, the RAF flew seven night raids, hitting Köln again on August 23-24. American *Viermots* flew no less than 32 sorties, including Köln (August 15) and Gelsenkirchen (August 26). I was traveling on furlough that day. When the train reached Bochum, air raid sirens howled, the train stopped, and all on board had to run to a bomb shelter near the station.

We spent two hours there, wondering whether it was Bochum again. It wasn't. It was Gelsenkirchen, twelve kilometers away. The impact of the bombing reverberated through the ground level and could clearly be felt in the shelter, an unsafe basement. I lived through an anxious time there. I wasn't used to being cooped up during an attack, confined in a closed space packed with fearful people. I was used to be in the open. In Reisholz we never went to cover. We stuck it out with the guns.

This was especially urgent when our city or a neighboring city was hammered. Because the fighter arm of the *Luftwaffe*, with too many fronts to cover and terribly outnumbered everywhere, was unable to stem the Allied air assaults, the Flak seemed the one and only line of defense. We stood and fired as well as we could. Even in Hüls, where we were useless with a 2cm against a high level attack that never came, and had to take to the foxholes when one threatened, we were still in the open. Our insubstantial foxholes were out in the "open." We fretted when we hunched there, but we preferred to have air and sky above us, hoping that our holes would not take a direct hit if it came to that. But in the Bochum shelter, the fear that emanated from the press of people, old and young, women and children mostly, was infectious. It lay over us like a cloud. I wondered how these helpless civilians could take it over and over on so many nights and not go crazy. They suffered their misery quietly, with expressionless faces, even the children. Life had become a condition of waiting, listening for the bomb that might come for you or might go elsewhere.

When the all-clear signal sounded we all trudged from the shelter and drifted to the station and back to board the abandoned train. It took some time until it started and slowly took us south. I disembarked in Düsseldorf.

That evening my parents told me my cousin Annie had been killed a few days before. There had been an alarm but no raid materialized. Only a few bombs had fallen, perhaps jettisoned by a *Viermot* crippled by Flak somewhere. One had struck a house on Benderstrasse in upper Gerresheim. In the first floor of the house was a store of the Reichelt chain of food stores. Annie was the manager. She and others there at the moment the bomb struck were buried in the wreckage. I remembered her as a friendly, out-going woman of about twenty-five, married to a *Luftwaffe* pilot. She was the last of the three children of my father's sister Anna to die. Willi was killed in action in Russia, Paul in Italy. The war was getting closer all the time. It was a melancholy weekend.

At the End, a Lightning. Back in Hüls the four of us buddies were transferred to *3. Zug* for a week, then to the *Vierlings-Zug*. The battery had already been a skeleton unit when we arrived back on January 18 1944. Now it seemed the battery was coming apart. We did the routine things expected of us but we were biding our time. We knew our enlistment orders for the *RAD* could arrive any time. We realized our time in Hüls was over but we also dreaded the consequences. We didn't know where we would go from here; each would go on his own. We would not be together any longer. Perhaps we might never see each other again.

The air war continued unabated. The RAF flew nine night attacks, including two on Königsberg. Königsberg in East Prussia? The ancient city of the German Teutonic Knights, built after their order removed from the Kingdom of Jerusalem during the Crusades. What was there to destroy? American *Viermots* flew no less than 32 sorties during the same period of nearly four weeks. They hit Düsseldorf again on September 9, a Saturday. We wondered once again what was left in our hometown that justified another attack. And what about our parents? We had no way to know if they were all right or even still alive. The uncertainty was torturous. We had one more class meeting on September 4, Monday. It was to be the last time. This episode in our lives was over, too.

The only significant event to directly affect us happened on September 17. There was considerable air activity. American fighter planes, Mustangs and Lightnings, filled the sky engaging German fighters, Me 109s and Fw 190s, in furious combat. We had manned the *Vierlings*. I sat in the gunner's seat, Wenner in the K 3 position on the gun to my left, Thei as K 4 on the right. We were ready if someone strayed into our range. The guns were aimed in the 9 o'clock position, covering the Hüls factory. We sat, watching the combat, the net of vapor trails across the sky. Nothing happened for a while. Then we heard the sound of aircraft at 3 o'clock. Swarms of Me 109s, with drop tanks under their bellies for long distance flight, hurried to the northwest, flying low and hugging features in the land. Lightnings and Mustangs swooped down on them. The Messerschmitts didn't give battle, but continued on their flights. We saw two shot down, bursting into flames as they hit the ground. As we watched we suddenly heard the *Fähnrich's* call from the command post between the revetments, "Enemy aircraft at 3 o'clock!"

I whirled the gun in that direction and then saw it. A single Lightning coming straight toward our position at a height of perhaps 500 meters (1500 feet). The pilot's attention must have focused on the distant engagement and not noticed the deadly danger in front of him. I had the plane in my sight as it came on, my feet on the fire pedals. The closer it came, the more eagerly we awaited permission to fire. But it didn't come. So the pretty, deadly bird flew over, unscathed. I followed it and swung the gun around as it went over us, covering it as it flew away. Only then did the section chief give the okay to shoot. I fired a burst with all four barrels but I undershot the plane. So did the others. I should have held lower. It wasn't our fault. It would have been a sure kill if we had been allowed to shoot as it was coming in. Either the *Fähnrich* was a coward or he didn't trust us to shoot straight, or both. Or he was afraid the plane would crash on our heads. In any case, this one got away and, maybe, that was best for all concerned. We learned later that an English Airborne Division had been dropped at Arnhem. That explained why the Messerschmitts had kept going in spite of being attacked. They were needed elsewhere.

This, it turned out, had been my last action as a *Flakhelfer*. Two days later a letter arrived from my parents with my enlistment order for the *RAD*. A few others received them the same day, the rest a day or two later. Each of us was ordered to different places. I was to report to a *RAD* camp in Eggebek in Schleswig-Holstein, near the border with Denmark. Thus, our Rethel *Gymnasium* group was broken up forever. We did not know who would replace us. The next crews were probably boys from secondary schools born in 1928. We turned our gear in, received our discharge papers and the rest of the pay due us, and set out for Recklinghausen and a train to Düsseldorf. One more phase of our lives had ended.

Before I left, I sneaked into one of the ammo bunkers and took three shells out: one armor-piercing (black top), one high explosive (yellow top), one incendiary (red tip on yellow top). This was the sequence with which they were rotated in magazines. I took them home with me and put them on the bookshelves in my room, as souvenirs, I guess. I can't tell you why. I don't know what I was thinking.

4

RAD Man

September 27-December 15 1944

Train to Hamburg. I spent three nights and two full days with my parents. During the first night, September 23-24, we went to the basement for two hours when the RAF bombed Dortmund and, closer, Neuss, southwest across the Rhine from us. There was no alarm the next two nights. My paren ts were glad my days in Hüls were over because of the constant threat of a major attack. They hoped my time with the *RAD* would be safe. After fifteen months as a *Flakhelfer* a mere twelve weeks in the *RAD* should not be too challenging.[1]

What they were worried about was what inevitably followed the *RAD*: the *Heer*. I didn't want to think that far.

The fact that I had to report to Eggebek was considered a blessing – because the camp was located in a rural area far away from population centers and other targets of the air war. But getting there was difficult and dangerous. I had to

---

1 The *RAD* (Reisarbeitsdienst – Reich Labor Service) was an invention of the Nazis after they came to power in 1933. Their system of militarizing German males was set up as a sequence of four stages: First stage was the *Jungvolk* ("Young People," the first branch of the Hitler Youth), composed of the ten to fourteen year olds. The second stage was the *Hitlerjugend* proper (the second branch of the Hitler Youth), the fourteen to eighteen year olds. The third stage was the *RAD*, the eighteen year olds. Following the *RAD*, young men were transferred into the Armed Forces. The *Jungvolk* wore black and brown uniforms. *Hitlerjugend* the same. *RAD* men wore brown uniforms.

Boys were first drafted into the *Jungvolk* and passed through successive stages. Nothing in the process was voluntary; passing through the stages was an obligation, considered a duty to the State. Only when transferred into the Armed Forces did inductees have a choice: they could volunteer for the *Heer*, *Luftwaffe*, *Kriegsmarine* and, after 1939, for the *Waffen-SS* (the military arm of the SS). All girls were inducted into an equivalent all-female organization of ten to fourteen year olds (BDM, *Bund Deutscher Mädchen*, League of German Girls), a girls' *Jungvolk*.

The *RAD*, from its inception, was a semi-military organization where men were housed in labor camps for a period of nine months preceding transfer into the Armed Forces. The task of the *RAD* was to provide physical labor for the "public good," such as building roads and bridges, drying swamps, clearing land for cultivation, constructing canals, etc. Pay was minimal. By 1944 the nine-month period of service had been reduced to twelve weeks of basic military training because the Armed Forces had begun to draft not only the eighteen year olds, but the seventeen year olds as well. The *RAD* had run out of men who could serve longer.

travel through the ruins of the Ruhr cities still under the threat of bombing as, for instance, Dortmund, hit again only nights before. And I must pass through other haunted places such as Paderborn, Hannover, and Hamburg.

We spent two good days together. In the early morning of September 26, I left my parents for the streetcar to the city and the Düsseldorf main railway station. It was still functioning, though surrounded by mountains of debris and twisted rails. I had taken a raincoat and a satchel filled with some personal items including a few books. I also took with me the memory of my parents' pale, distressed faces, their huge eyes.

I had to wait, but eventually boarded a train that would go as far as Hannover. From there I had to look for a train to take me to Hamburg. Train travel in our part of Germany had become hazardous and erratic. Schedules were irregular, depending on the exigencies of wartime. That trains still ran at all, in spite of the heavy bombing, was a near miracle. The effort to make it happen was gargantuan but it was done and it worked.

Again, I traveled through the apocalyptic, desolated landscape that was the Ruhr. Near the little town of Herdecke, twelve kilometers south of Dortmund, the trains suddenly halted and all passengers were ordered out. Sirens screamed everywhere. An American air raid was striking Osnabrück a hundred kilometers to the northeast. And additional bomber formations were closing in from the northwest, their target unknown. The train was emptied and passengers hurried to bomb shelters, simple cellars in buildings near the railroad. They were already filled. We sat crammed together, all civilians, nearly all old people and women with children on their knees. We sat quietly, listening. I didn't think this place was in real danger, but what about Dortmund? When we heard the sound of heavy bombing from far away we knew it was too far to be Dortmund. Still we had to wait until sirens gave the all-clear signal. Then we crowded the train again. We were informed that the city of Hamm had been struck, 35 kilometers to the northeast.

This time the recent Dortmund attack had not affected the rail system. In the western part of the city fires still smoldered; we saw and smelled the smoke. We went slow through the badly damaged city, but we went. In Düsseldorf I had noted that *Vierlings* had been added to the front and rear of our train. I would have felt more comfortable if I had been given a chance to man one of them. I didn't know who the gunners were, *Flakhelfer* or soldiers. It seemed that low-level attacks by Allied fighter planes were becoming a real threat.

Nothing happened to us, though, and the train made Hannover in the early evening. Along the way, little towns and villages appeared untouched. Paderborn showed plenty of ruins, but Hannover, attacked so many times, was devastated. In the station I found out that the train to Hamburg would leave in the morning. I spent the night on a cot in a shelter, a collection place for traveling soldiers and persons like me. I was admitted after my papers were checked by *Feldpolizei*. On the four cots next to me were soldiers going on furlough to Hamburg and towns nearby. They had come all the way from Greece. They had little leather bags among their gear with leaf tobacco grown there, and they treated them like treasures. They were in high spirits and passed a bottle of ouzo, offering me a drink and a cigarette. I gladly accepted. Our happy hour time came to an end when a military policeman told us to quit.

The train arrived before 7 A.M. and left quickly, as if trying to get away from the city. We covered the 140 kilometers to Hamburg in about three hours, gratefully, without incident. The *Viermots* must have been busy elsewhere.

Hamburg was a frightful sight. Blocks on end with fire-blackened façades and the empty holes of windows behind which interiors had been converted to mounds of rubble. The Alster was an oily, dark swamp. The Old Testament's Gomorrah had truly found a modern match. There still was a railway station, though, and three hours later I got a train north to Flensburg, on the border with Denmark. South of Flensburg I left the train at Eggebek, nothing more than a hamlet on the railroad. I walked to the *RAD* camp a few kilometers away. It was late afternoon. I showed my enlistment order and was directed to headquarters. There I presented both my enlistment order and *Flakhelfer* discharge papers and was supplied with the accoutrements of a *RAD* man, including fatigues and dress uniform. Both were in brown color, "the color of shit," as my old friends in the Gerresheim blue-collar neighborhood used to say.

Eggebek. The camp was an arrangement of wooden barracks around an open square with a swastika flag on the pole in the center. Perhaps 400 boys were garrisoned here along with perhaps a dozen *RAD* "leaders." In principle the *RAD* was an extension of the Hitler Youth, and the terms for its office-holders were copied from that organization. So they were called *Führer* ("leaders").

The leaders at Eggebek saw themselves as "Hitlermen." Without exception they were fanatical Nazis, uncompromising, acting tough. These were the men who trained us in weapons' use, infantry tactics and long distance marches with weapons and the usual infantry gear. We didn't think any one of them had combat experience. There were only a few German machine-guns, but we fired them regularly on the shooting range. We were basically a rifle battalion. Our rifles were Krag rifles, captured Norwegian Army rifles of a different caliber that used a loading gate instead of a clip. Their performance was as good as that of the Mauser 98 model used by our *Heer*.

Discipline was excessive and ruthlessly enforced. The slightest infraction perceived by a leader was punished with a hundred push-ups or a latrine-cleaning, or both. From *Flakhelfer*, I had stepped into another world. Never in the batteries had an officer or non-commissioned officer even considered treating us the way these *RAD Bonzen* (bigwigs) did. I wondered what their military experience had been, if any. As a consequence of their attitude and our treatment, morale among the troops was low. We were listless and lethargic. We did what we were ordered but without interest. The *Bonzen* were despised by most of us except for a small segment of dedicated Hitler Youth. We had to be careful of them. There were a few ex-*Flakhelfer*, including Micha (his nickname), one of the Rethel boys who had been with me in Bad Einsiedel, Reisholz and Hüls. In Reisholz he had served in the *Mess-Staffel*. He stayed aloof in Eggebek, keeping to himself and to buddies in his barrack, some of whom belonged to the Hitler Youth wing. He traded with me, however, his cigarette ration for bread from my food ration.

Eggebek was located in the northern part of Germany's most northern province, Schleswig-Holstein. The province was framed in the west by the North Sea and in the east by the Baltic Sea. The camp was 24 kilometers south of the Danish border, 30 kilometers east of the Wattenmeer of the North Sea and 41 kilometers west of the Baltic Sea. Flat farming country surrounded us. It seemed like we were in the no-mans' land of the war, but we weren't. Close to the west side of the camp was a large *Luftwaffe* airfield with a military role we quickly came to understand. The airfield was the base of a fighter wing of Me 109s placed there to intercept American *Viermots* on raids against cities such as Kiel and Lübeck on the Baltic coast.

The airfield was also a base for He 111 two-engined bombers that had outlived their original use because of inadequate speed and their high vulnerability. A new purpose had been found for them. I don't know how many were stationed there, but every night a few were fitted with V-1 rockets. They took off for the dark sky over the North Sea where they released the rockets toward targets in England. The whole operation was cloaked in secrecy but we couldn't help seeing what went on. We never saw how the V-1s were loaded on the He 111s frames in the hangars, but we saw the old birds roar across the runway before they lifted off and disappeared into the night. The V-1 sitting atop an He 111 was a strange sight. Later in the night the planes returned, one after another.

After I had seen this spectacle a few times it dawned on me why the *RAD* camp might have been situated where it was. Were we considered a force emplaced to protect the airfield in case of a commando raid by enemy forces or some other threat? Was this why we trained so hard infantry tactics? I never found an answer to this question, and the *Bonzen* never talked about it.

There was a lot of activity at the airfield. Me 109s often took off and returned during daylight, sometimes shot up. No nightfighters were stationed there. The airfield was surrounded by wooden towers and revetments with light Flak, 2cm and 3.7cm guns. There were no heavies, 8.8cm, 10.5cm, or 12.8cm guns. We never got close to one of the *Züge* but I was sure that *Flakhelfer* were involved. Perhaps all the guns were manned by them the way we had done in Hüls.

Once a few of us were able to sneak to the edge of the airfield where a single Messerschmitt fighter plane sat in cover. There was no one around. Perhaps the plane was not in combat readiness. We walked around it and admired the sleek bird. It was painted light blue underneath, sides and upper part of the fuselage were camouflaged with grey bands and dots. A scoreboard on the rudder showed nine rectangular markings indicating nine victories. Under each wing a cannon of a caliber a bit larger than 2cm was fitted inside a gondola.

One after another, we climbed into the pilot's seat. When I sat in the cabin I was shocked by how narrow and confined it was. From within this tight space a pilot would fly his machine straight into the guns of a bomber box, gauge the distance, fire a burst, and pull up over a Fortresses nose? I gained a deep respect for all the fighter pilots who had to fight in such cramped quarters.

One memorable event occurred a week after my arrival. For a reason I don't remember, the whole battalion was punished. We were ordered to wear our dress uniforms and assemble on the square. It had rained most of the day and deep puddles of water were everywhere. The top *Bonze* ordered us to form up in column and marched us through the worst puddles, and back, and again. Every time we got to a puddle he gave the command "Stechschritt" (goose-step). It was the first and only time I was ordered to do this. The exercise lasted for over half an hour and ended when we were covered with watery mud from boots to upper torsos. When we were dirtied enough, we were dismissed and ordered to assemble 45 minutes later for inspection. Our soiled uniforms had to be thoroughly cleaned first, and they were.

Had a commando raid come then, and had we been called into combat, the *Bonzen* might have survived the enemy, but perhaps not a couple of Krags.

The Raid. Life became routine. Wake-up was at 7 A.M. Cross-country running, rain or shine. Cleaning up in washrooms. Dressing and readying our bed and locker for possible inspection. Flag-raising. Marching to the mess hall for breakfast. Weapons instruction. Political indoctrination. Exercises. Shooting on the range with machine-gun and rifle. Or a longer march with weapons and gear. Lunch in the mess hall. Weapon cleaning. A break. More instruction. Supper. Finally an end. Light out at 9 P.M.

I got along with my new comrades though I missed the buddies I had been with as *Flakhelfer* for so long. Some of the guys around me were all right. Some were not. Most were in military training for the first time. Some were sissies. Others were uninformed, uneducated, and the victims of years of propaganda. In many ways we were all victims. We all tried to learn how to survive in the war. The *Bonzen* were trying to teach us, but what did they really know? Did they think that Nazi ideology would protect us?

Some of us, the handful of *Flakhelfer*, had already learned something the rest didn't know. It made no difference. We were in the same boat. Our experience did not count. We were regarded with suspicion because we were considered different, students of secondary schools. Most of the others only had an elementary school education. That didn't matter to me. But it was important to them; they were wary of us few. It should not have been that way, but it was. We had already served the guns in hard times, but that was beyond their personal experience.

I often felt lonely. I found solace in the books I had brought with me. For a time they let me slip into a different world.

Sometimes we shot at targets from foxholes as part of our training. But there were no foxholes around the barracks, no bomb shelters. I wondered about that. In Hüls, foxholes had been our last resort when the possibility of a major raid threatened. Here, there was nothing for our safety. Why?

I wondered. Hüls, a major chemical factory devoted to the German war effort in producing chemical weapons, was left alone by the Allies. So was Eggebek airfield from which V-1 attacks were unleashed against England. In addition, the fighter wing operating from the same airfield was an obstacle to the Allied air war, and thus a target. Why were places such as these spared when crippled population centers on the Ruhr, the Rhine, and elsewhere, hit dozens and dozens of times and reduced to almost nothing, were still under attack? I called on my *Flakhelfer* experience from Reisholz and Hüls, where I had seen cities burn around us almost night after night. None of this made any sense.

Late on the morning of October 17 the battalion was again on the shooting range. We were used to the frequent taking off and landing of fighter planes, but suddenly we heard a different sound, the growling of aircraft engines of lots of planes flying low and close together. We stood and listened. The light Flak around the airfield opened up. And then we saw them. They hugged the flat countryside, aiming at the airfield or targets there, flying perhaps 200 meters (600 feet) above ground. Fighter planes in gaudy colors with strange markings rapidly closed in. I recognized them from our study sessions on aircraft in Hüls. Spitfires! English! Their cannons let loose. For a few seconds, guns from the ground and the towers combined to make a tremendous noise. Then the Spitfires streaked by the airfield command post, barely missing it, and disappeared. Smoke billowed from a number of places on the airfield. Something had been hit. Someone pointed to the northwest. A number of farm buildings were aflame in the direction from which the Spitfires had approached. Our Flak had missed and had hit farms behind them. We never learned what damage the attack had done to German aircraft on the airfield and in hangars. We were told two of the raiders were shot down, both crashing on the runway.

It was the only raid on the Eggebek airfield during the weeks I was there.

Waiting. The *RAD* dress uniforms we had received upon arrival represented an empty promise. We wore them once when a high-ranking *Bonze* came for an inspection, and the time the battalion was marched through mud as punishment for an infraction most of us knew nothing about. We were never allowed to leave the camp, but then, where could we have gone except to visit the Holstein milk cows that grazed on pastures all around us.

Training went on relentlessly although Allied ground forces had reached the German border in the west and the Russians were approaching East Prussia. The ancient city of Aachen had fallen in late October. From Aachen to Cologne and the Rhine River was only 60 kilometers, to Düsseldorf, 75. How long would it take the Americans to cover that distance? What were we doing in Eggebek? Perhaps this would be over soon?

What little we knew came from the letters parents sent us. My parents, who wrote regularly, tried to be positive and didn't mention the disasters that were befalling us everywhere. But I knew how to read between the lines and I understood how they felt. The *Bonzen* kept us in the dark, responding to the flow of bad news they alone had access to with stiffer and stiffer training, as if we alone would be the answer to all problems. Of course, the demise of the Third Reich would be their own demise, too. But what about us boys? The "wonder weapons" that Hitler had promised turned out to be the V-1 and V-2 rockets, but these had not changed anything. We watched the V-1 go *Huckepack* (piggy- back) on the He 111s in the dark of night – not a sign of confidence.

We were afraid, distressed. Only the Hitler Youth wings of true believers still expected a German "final victory." The rest of us got a brief respite in our condition when the top *Bonze* from our camp, the commandant, a sinister hard-liner, was arrested by what we thought were *Gestapo* and was taken away. We learned he was accused of corruption, selling food from our camp supplies on the black market for personal gain.

Such wartime transgressions were punished in the Nazi state with the death sentence. The Hitler Youth wing remained silent about the incident. Not the rest of us. The hypocrite! He had been in a cushy job far from danger, training us to fight for the "Führer" and the Fatherland to the last, and then used his position to enrich himself. Many of us felt he would get what he deserved.

In a letter dated November 8, my parents told me that Düsseldorf had been bombed again during the night of November 2-3. I was sure they mentioned it only to calm my fears for them in case I had heard about it. They could not know that in Eggebek we knew nothing of the continuing air war because we were deprived of all information. Gerresheim, at least, had been spared again.

Because we got modest rations of cigarettes as *RAD* men, I had become a smoker. As kids earlier, we had sometimes puffed in the woods or other secluded spots. They were cigarettes we had taken from our homes without our parents' knowledge. Those pranks had been fun, although we didn't enjoy smoking; at that time we usually threw up or felt dizzy. In Eggebek we got past that and joined the ranks of the adults.

Time passed and we all got more and more restless. We knew what was ahead for us. We were finally informed that on December 14 our battalion would be disbanded. We would await our draft notices for the *Heer* at home. The morning of December 14 came. For a last time we stood in formation on the square and watched the flag with the swastika being lowered. Returning our *RAD* uniforms and gear took some time. Singly and in groups we walked to the Eggebek railway station, leaving the *RAD* experience behind us forever.

Train to Düsseldorf. The trip home turned out to be a nightmare. Four hundred boys tried to get home, most to distant places like me. Why had we been sent halfway across Germany to Eggebek when there were *RAD* camps closer to home?

From Schleswig, a city southeast of Eggebek, half of us went to Kiel and Lübeck and other places on the Baltic Sea coast. The other half went south to Hamburg. It was not easy. We had to wait for trains, and when they finally came they were already crowded.

Arriving in Hamburg late, those of us who planned to go south through Hannover and beyond got a nasty surprise. We were told the railway line through Hannover had been closed for the time being. A heavy air raid had hit the city once more, just an hour before we got to Hamburg. Damage to the rail system was said to be severe. The only route for those of us who needed to go to the Ruhr cities or the Rhineland was through Bremen, and from there through Osnabrück and Münster to Dortmund. Many of us went to Bremen, getting there in the dark. No train left for the south that night. Those that had to continue went to shelters that existed in or near every major railway station.

In the morning we saw some soldiers and civilians standing around a radio. I and a few others of our bunch went to listen. We heard that this very morning a major operation called the Ardennes Offensive had started in the west. German armored divisions were advancing into Belgium on a broad front. The announcer's voice was cautiously optimistic. He reported early successes. We stood with mixed feelings, in silence. We looked at each other. Faces were calm, thoughtful. They seemed to say: "All right, our soldiers are on the attack again. If they give the Amis a beating, what will that do? In the end we cannot win. They, on the other side, have everything. We have almost nothing left." No one said it aloud but it seemed to me that everyone was thinking it.

The group of listeners slowly broke up. We ex-*RAD* guys went to the information desk to ask about a train connection south to Osnabrück and Dortmund. We were told there would be none that day. The official shrugged and said that the military had ordered the rail line closed to civilian travel. Perhaps, he said, tomorrow traffic might resume.

We spent the day and another night in Bremen. We never left the station. Bremen was as badly hit by the bombings as were the Ruhr cities. We had seen enough destruction. Outside, dark clouds and heavy rain. A grim day and night. We worried. In the morning the rail line was reopened and there actually was a train, hastily put together with cars worn from use and misuse. The train actually got away without incident toward Osnabrück. Overcrowded, it rolled on through Osnabrück and Münster and reached Dortmund. We almost felt we had made it home. The day was rainy and dark, dark clouds hanging low, hardly moving, closing the sky on the *Viermots* and their little brothers, Mustangs and Lightnings and Thunderbolts. We felt lucky. The train ended in Dortmund and the last seven of us from Düsseldorf and Neuss had to wait a couple of hours for a slow train to get us to our hometowns on Sunday evening. I barely made the last streetcar to Gerresheim. It began to snow as we pulled away from the railway station. The snow became heavy when I reached my parents and home.

5

Interlude

December 17 1944-January 5 1945

Home. My mother embraced me wordlessly. Even my father, who rarely allowed himself to show emotion, gave me a handshake and a half embrace. We looked at each other. They both appeared worn and sad, but their eyes were alive. I didn't know how they saw me. We only had a short time to talk. If bad weather had kept the American bombers away during the day, it did nothing to deter the RAF. Their Lancasters and Halifaxes could be relied upon to come at night during any weather, as long as they could take off in England. And that night was no different. We spent two hours in the basement shelter until near midnight when the all-clear signals howled.

I already felt odd in the basement. At first I thought it might be because the neighbors stared at me. I could understand their curiosity, but this was too much. I was not used to civilians anymore, having spent so much time in the company of uniformed men and boys. I quickly became hostile. But I also felt a burning agitation in my body, a sudden surge of heat. There was a pain in my throat and it became painful to swallow. I looked at the floor below me, trying to adjust. My mother noticed that something was wrong. I could see the worry in her eyes as she put a hand on my shoulder. Then she placed both hands on my temples. "You have a fever," she said. I started to get up but my father said, "wait a little, this will be over soon." I held out, but when the sirens screamed and we could leave I fell into bed.

Because of the fever my mother sat by me and applied an old folk medicine technique, the only treatment at hand. She wrapped my calves with wet, cold compresses, "to draw the fever out." I wasn't sure it would help but I was in no condition to argue. When the compresses warmed up my father went and freshened them with cold water. I was shaking badly. Lymph nodes under my lower jaw were swollen. My throat was raw. My parents agreed, "It's tonsillitis." I had had it once before when I was younger.

When I woke up in the morning, Dr. Strunk stood at my bed. He was our family physician who had his practice in his big house two blocks away. My mother had rushed to bring him. He checked me out, looked at my red, swollen tonsils and confirmed the diagnosis, "Tonsillitis." Not a serious disease. The only medication he was able to prescribe was a foul smelling bluish liquid I had to gargle with about twice every hour. My mother got it from a pharmacy and I went to work with it. I spent four days in bed, but recovered from the dead on December 21.

I felt a little weak but in good spirits. Perhaps the tonsillitis had been the product and aftermath of the turmoil in Eggebek. Dr. Strunk did one wonderful thing for us. He took my draft notice and he mailed it to the *WBK*, the *Wehrbezirks-Kommando*, in Düsseldorf, with a medical report stating that I was not capable of military service due to a severe illness. My parents knew the doctor as a man opposed to the regime. We thought he had exaggerated my condition. My parents were relieved because I would be safe and at home for a while.

The air raid on the night of my arrival had been on Duisburg, 25 kilometers north of us. On the night of December 21-22 it was Köln again. It could have been us. It seemed that I was back in the old rut after a brief respite in Eggebek. There was no point in brooding about it. Instead we concentrated on Christmas, a few days away. There were Christmas trees available in a nursery in lower Gerresheim, and on Friday, December 22, my father and I went to get one. It was a beautiful fir, about six feet tall. I carried it home through the snow, handling it like a baby. My mother stood it in a bucket of water in our empty garage for the night. The following morning I brought it upstairs and into the living room. My father and I put it up and decorated it. We put on the electric lights and the old, fragile glass ornaments that had been in our family from great-grandmother's time in colors of gold and silver and red and green. While doing so we each smoked a cigarette and had a small glass of brandy. It wasn't like old times but it was pretty good.

Ah, Christmas. On Saturday, December 23, the day before Christmas Eve, I sat by the kitchen table watching my mother prepare *Spekulatius* cookies. Originally the dough required butter and almonds, but there were no butter and almonds. She had margarine, flower, some hazelnuts, and the necessary spices from years past. When all the ingredients were included, the dough was kneaded and compacted into a ball. I got to test a piece before she put the ball on a covered plate and placed it on the windowsill outside in the cold. It had to rest a few hours before baking could begin. Next to the *Spekulatius* ball hung the naked corpse of a rabbit, ready for the pot. My father had gotten it from one of his men at the machine shop.

I stayed while my mother prepared the Christmas cake. It could not be *Stollen*. It would be a simple cake with dried fruit from our trees. I watched an experienced baker at work and ate some of her dried apple slices. When she put the finished mixture in its tin mold into the oven, I showed her my appreciation and then walked over to join my father in the living room.

We had a good day together. We talked about past times we wanted to remember. We didn't talk about the war. We knew my time with them was limited. The three of us hoped I would not be sent for *Heer* training in the east. Then I would go to the Russian Front. If I reported to some place west or nearby, I might get sent to the Western Front. Of two bad choices the latter seemed by far the best. But, perhaps, the war might be over before my training was finished. These thoughts hung over us like weights, regardless of how hard we tried to push them away. We sat by the lit tree while outside snowflakes danced against the windows. We were together but we felt alone. There was no alarm during the night. Perhaps the RAF also needed to celebrate the ancient message of peace.

The Christmas Eve Mass on December 24 was again held during the late afternoon. My parents and I walked to St. Margaretha in deep snow. The inside of the basilica was as I remembered it from last year. The nativity scene was in place. Musicians played a jubilant J.S. Bach Oratorio, a message from another world. I listened to the sounds and voices that seemed to open a crack into heaven beyond the present, something eternal. The crowd around us was like last year's. Women, children, old people, a few soldiers, some with crutches. But it was Bach who reigned, his music something to turn to in desperate times. The sermon was short. The reading of the list of the recently fallen a perversion: "Für Führer, Volk und Vaterland." We took the meaning and the power of the oratory with us when we went home. There was nothing to say.

But at home we went again into the presence of the lights on the tree. One more Christmas together. There were no presents. To be there, the three of us together, was the gift.

Miss Jonen. Dr. Strunk's letter to the *WBK* delivered a surprising result. On December 27, I received a formal statement from that office in the mail. It said that my draft order had been "canceled until further notice." I was granted a bit more time.

After I read the letter I went to visit the city library Unter den Eichen and the librarian, Miss Jonen. She was in her early sixties now, grey-haired, a little bent, but the eyes behind the glasses were as sharp and probing as ever. We greeted each other with a fond handshake. She had been my guide into the wondrous world of books from the time I had learned to read. Through my mother she had supplied me with books in Reisholz and Hüls, and broken more than a few rules doing so. But she kept me reading, and reading worthwhile and stimulating books. We talked for a while about personal matters. She and another elderly lady had been restacking books. On top of the pile in front of her was a thick, large-format volume. I looked at it and she said with a smile, "Egyptian history, art, and religion." She nodded. "Perhaps you should look at it. Take it home. Your mother can return it." She knew how to tempt me.

I took the book with me and never regretted it. This was a marvelous book, perhaps what I needed. I immersed myself in the wonders that had been Old Egypt. This book began with the Pre-Dynastic Period and carried through to the Ptolemaic Period and the Roman Conquest. Most fascinating to me, because of the great quality of the works in art and architecture, was the time from the Old Kingdom to the New Kingdom, a period lasting eleven hundred years. Eleven hundred years out of over three thousand years of Egyptian history!

My grandmother, the "Kleine Oma," once opened my mind and my heart to the beauty of the world, to the magic of far-away places, the exotic, the strange and wonderful. My mother had deftly supported my clumsy probes into these areas after my grandmother died, and then Miss Jonen had become my knowledgeable adviser and helper. Now, in this volume, I was looking into something utterly different, breathtaking, totally removed from the contemporary misery of life. There was something else in these paintings, these figures of gods and heroes and sacred animals that stood against mortality and the profane.

So I lost myself in the book. There were three night alarms during these nights. On December 27-28, the RAF bombed Leverkusen, on 28-29, Mönchen-Gladbach, on 30-31, Köln – all more or less in our neighborhood. I took the Egypt volume with me into the basement shelter and read and took notes in a special notebook, ignoring the fury of the Flak heavies and the distant thunder of the carpets of bombs. My parents understood and were happy for me. The neighbors in the shelter kept watching me, perhaps wondering at my indifference to what was happening around us and the intensity of my reading. They didn't dare to ask me about it.

For the next ten days I read and took notes and made drawings, filling over half of the notebook. Later I took it into the war with me as sort of an antidote against the cruelty threatening to overwhelm us. I lost the notebook after I no longer needed it.

In the afternoon of New Year's Eve, American *Viermots* bombed Vohwinkel, a suburb of Wuppertal fourteen kilometers east of Gerresheim. We heard the bomber stream and the impact of blockbusters from the basement shelter where I held on to Egyptian mythology. But the evening, clear and cold, was peaceful. My parents and I had some wine and toasted the arrival of the New Year, wishing that it would bring something good.

Eyes. On January 2 1945, our local newspaper was full of news about a massive raid by hundreds of German fighter-bombers on Allied airfields in Holland, Belgium and France. The paper called Operation *Bodenplatte* a great success, a stunning set-back for Allied air forces. If it proved true, there would be a lull in the bombing campaign. We would have to wait and see.

In the early afternoon that day I went into the city for a movie, the first time in a long time. I took streetcar No. 3 to Grafenberg, then No. 9 to Graf-Adolf-Strasse past the railway station. Most of this street near the Düsseldorf center was in ruins. Before the war there had been four movie theaters on a section of that street alone. Now only one was left standing, damaged, but still operating. It doesn't matter what the movie was; nothing remarkable. It was a brief escape from reality. But something important happened afterward.

When the show was over I walked to Graf-Adolf Square to catch the No. 9 for the ride back. While I waited I met a kid from Rethel School I knew, a year younger than I, now a *Flakhelfer* in a battery north of the city. We talked a little. He asked me how I was. I said, "Good." I just said it automatically. It didn't mean anything and it wasn't even true. Then I looked into the face of a woman standing next to us. She had heard me. She stared at me with huge, empty eyes.

She was a middle-aged woman, clothed in a drab, tattered coat, with a face into which sorrow and sadness had cut deep lines. Who knew what she had suffered, whom or how many she had lost. And there I stood, rather well-dressed in an old but fairly good trench coat, well-fed by my mother. The woman couldn't know me, that often I might feel as she felt. Perhaps, I thought, she saw me as a profiteer, some weasel who knew how to stay away from danger, somehow sheltered from the misery of others.

I felt like a heel, a coward. Why was I still here? All my buddies were in the war, all the younger people I had known, many already dead. Everything was collapsing and here I was, biding my time. The eyes of this woman seemed to accuse me. She probably didn't mean anything by the way she looked at me, or didn't understand how it made me feel. But suddenly I was ashamed that I was hiding. I had to go where the others were, regardless of what happened.

I could not forget her eyes, all the other eyes. Next morning, when a sergeant from the *WBK* arrived at our door and asked me if I was fit for service, I said yes. Had I let my mother answer the door while I played sick in bed, Dr. Strunk might have bailed me out one more time. Perhaps, but I could no longer accept that.

Markings on a Tree. I went by streetcar to the huge, partly destroyed building at the edge of Old Town that housed the *WBK*. In the entrance hall sat a *Waffen-SS* sergeant behind a desk, waiting for kids like me. I had to walk past him to get where I needed to go. He got up and said, "You are coming to us, aren't you?"

He meant that I should volunteer for the *Waffen-SS*: I said, "No. I am a reserve officer candidate in the *Heer*."

I had to show him my papers. "What branch do you want to go to?" he asked.

"Panzer," I said.

"We have Panzer, too. We have better Panzer than the *Heer*. You can become an officer in the *Waffen-SS*, too."

I said, "No. I want to be *Heer*."

He had to let me go. If I had not had papers documenting that I had already been accepted as a reserve officer's candidate, he would have pulled me into the *Waffen-SS*. I knew that many kids who did not have my credentials were hi-jacked into the *Waffen-SS*, mostly harmless kids who were later treated as fanatical Nazis by the Western Allies and the Russians.

At the *Heer* desk, they ignored my wish to be sent to an armored unit. Instead, I received orders to report the next day to the Sagan *Kaserne* in Wuppertal-Elberfeld, and the *Grenadier-Ersatz-und-Ausbildungs-Bataillon 464*, 1st Company. It wasn't Panzer but Grenadier, and perhaps that was for the best.

My parents did not take the news well. I knew they wouldn't. But they were glad that I was sent to Wuppertal and not some place in the east. My father and I had one preparation to make we felt was important. We went to the front of the house and marked one of the old trees with knife cuts, crosswise. We agreed that, if my parents had to leave the house for one reason or another, but were still alive, they would leave information at the foot of the tree so that I would find them when I came back. We didn't say if I came back.

We spent our last evening together in a grave and thoughtful mood. We tried to be upbeat but it was hard. There was no alarm that night. I didn't sleep much, and I am sure my parents didn't either.

In the dark, early morning of January 5 I said good-bye to my mother. She tried hard not to cry. My father walked with me to the streetcar station on the corner of Schönau-Strasse, a couple of blocks away.

I took my old diary with me in which I had recorded my *Flakhelfer* and *RAD* times, the new notebook on Egyptian mythology, history and art, and R.C. Sherriff's World War I play, *Journey's End*. We had not been able to finish reading it in Bad Einsiedel but I had done so in Hüls. I took it for the English text and because it had meaning for me. My own journey's end seemed to loom somewhere just before me.

I did not want my father to go farther than the streetcar station. I hated good-byes. We hardly spoke on the short walk. He knew better than I where I was going; he had been there. He was solemn, turned within himself. We did not know if we would see each other again. The streetcar came. We looked into each other's eyes. What do you see when you see? We might have embraced briefly, but I don't remember. I got in and the streetcar went away. The car was filled with people. I took a last look. How did he make it back to my mother on that morning?

6

Grenadier

January 5-March 28 1945

Sagan *Kaserne*. The twin cities of Wuppertal-Elberfeld, about 30 kilometers east of Düsseldorf, stretched along a narrow valley beside the Wupper River. Slopes on both sides rose sharply to plateaus above. It was a perfect setting for the demolition of a city with blockbusters. Pressure from the explosions intensified in the tight space as they bounced against the slopes and were thrown back. The English knew all about this, and their bomber crews did what they had been ordered to do. Perhaps they saw this place as another Sodom, one of many. The result was that the twin cities had been about 70-80 % destroyed when I arrived at the shell of a railway station.

I was one of a few people who left the train. I asked directions to the military base. A late-comer, once again. I walked past blackened ruins up a winding road to the plateau south of the city. Before me lay the Sagan *Kaserne*, a sprawling complex of stone buildings for military personnel with associated armories, motor vehicle parks, training areas, shooting ranges, etc. This huge aggregation of structures, one of the premier military training facilities in the region, had never been touched by the Allied air campaign. I hoped that it would remain so. But it did appear that Bomber Command preferred the twin cities, an oft-visited target, to the military base.

I reported at the main gate and was sent to Headquarters of Grenadier E and A Battalion 464, one of a number of such headquarters. I showed my papers to a sergeant who passed me on to 1st Company. The staff consisted of a sergeant-major, two lance- corporals and two *Wehrmacht* Helferinnen – women in uniform assigned to office work. They were in their early thirties dressed in white blouses and skirts in *Heer* field grey. No officer was in sight. I approached the sergeant-major who sat behind a desk and handed him my papers. He looked me over and said, "You are late." I explained. He nodded. He shuffled some papers on his desk.

I had time to look him over. He was a thin man of medium height perhaps 40 years old. He had a chest full of medals. Most distinguished for an infantryman was the *Nahkampf-Spange* (Close Combat Badge) over his left breast pocket. This badge was granted by the *Heer* in bronze, silver, and gold. The gold one was for 50 days of close combat, obviously a rare decoration. His was gold. This was not the regular sergeant- major type. A surprise.

While I was contemplating that he looked at me with a rather wooden face and the ghost of a smile. "You go to 2nd Platoon, 1st Company," he said. He made a gesture with his hand that could have meant, "Good luck." He called one of the lance-corporals and he took me to rooms where I was outfitted with the whole range of equipment a grenadier was supposed to need. He helped me carry it and led me to the second floor of a building where the company was quartered. The room was empty when we arrived. The guys were out on training. I picked one of the few unoccupied cots and the empty locker next to it. I changed from civilian clothes into army fatigues and stored my equipment in the locker. Then I sat down and checked the Mauser 98 carbine I had been issued. I hefted it to my shoulder. It weighed about the same as the Krag I had used in Eggebek. I worked the bolt action and looked through the barrel. Well oiled. There were two windows in the room. I looked out of one to the square below. This was it, the place where I would become a soldier.

Becoming a Grenadier. 2nd Platoon was one of three that made up the company. A platoon consisted of three squads, each led by a corporal eighteen to nineteen years old. Each of them had combat experience. The platoon was led by a sergeant. A platoon comprised a total of 31 men, including the non-commissioned officers. The company, with a lieutenant as its commanding officer, numbered about 95 men. The total number in the battalion, consisting of three companies, was roughly 285 men.

Compared with earlier compositions in the German Army, these companies were weak in manpower, and that made for a weak battalion. But all through the German Army of 1944-1945, the strengths of units had drastically declined due to losses in battle. We were no exception. The *Heer* tried to overcome the deficit in manpower with more advanced weapons. Each of our squads was equipped with a machine-gun (MG) 42 that had a rate of fire of 1,200 rounds per minute. Thus each platoon had three MG 42s, each company nine, and the battalion, a total of 27. The riflemen, because of the extremely high rate of fire of these guns, were required to support them. Each carried loads of machine-gun ammunition in metal boxes and wore extra belts of rounds around their necks when going into combat. In addition, each sergeant and corporal carried a *Sturmgewehr* (a new and superior type of machine pistol), also increasing firepower. I myself preferred my rifle, a weapon I had long been familiar with.

The grenadiers in our battalion were generally seventeen years old. We all came from a region within a radius of 50 to 70 kilometers from Sagan *Kaserne*. Thus, we came from the Rhineland, from the Ruhr, and the hilly country around Wuppertal. All of us had witnessed major cities burned to the ground. A difference from my *RAD* experience was that no Hitler Youth believers were among us. Perhaps those guys had gonc to the *Waffen-SS* from the various *WBK*s where they registered. There was a sizeable number of ex-*Flakhelfer* among us.

We were a bunch such as the German Army had never known before. But then, never before had kids our age been prepared for combat. Having been trained for military work from *Jungvolk* times on, when we were ten years old, we were not bad in military craft and did well on the shooting range. But we believed in nothing anymore. The rhetoric of the Nazis, of nearly everyone in authority, we had found to be lies, empty promises. During the day, while on exercises or at the shooting range, we saw the vapor trails of American bombers and fighter planes crisscrossing the sky. Many a night we rushed to the basement because of an air raid alarm, wondering if it would be us this time. Sometimes we heard the faint clamor of heavy bombing, such as on January 10 when Düsseldorf was hit again, or the day following when Krefeld was struck. And Duisburg, January 22-23, Neuss on January 23, Köln and Duisburg, January 28, Dortmund on February 4, and Düsseldorf once more on February 20-21. And so it continued. In February we had to get used to hearing the distant, steady rumble of artillery fire from the west as American spearheads were moving toward the Rhine, our river. The war was getting closer, coming our way, unstoppable.

I think there was not one among us kids who believed that the war could still be won. I was not sure whether the officers and non-coms thought otherwise; I doubted it. They were caught with us in the same trap. We had become totally nihilistic. We trusted only each other, no one else. We expected to be thrown into the great grinder. When volunteers were requested to serve in the one-man torpedoes (more or less a suicide commando), a number of us registered. I was one of them. We wanted to get it over with. We were all seriously messed up. A little later this appeal was canceled. There was no sea space left in which to launch one-man-torpedoes against Allied ships before Normandy or Antwerp.

During all that time our training continued at a furious pace, perhaps to wear us out and prevent us from thinking critically about the condition of our world. What we did was more of the same things we had done in Eggebek and elsewhere, only more seriously: long marches (40 kilometers) with weapons and heavy packs; shooting rifles, MG 42s, *Sturmgewehre*, and the *Panzerfaust*. And there was hand grenade throwing, cleaning weapons, disassembling and reassembling them – all the exercises a sod infantryman is supposed to master before engaging in what the ancient philosopher called "the art of war." By that time, however, we had long ago learned that war was not an art but a dirty, deadly affair. Our chances to survive were very limited.

I exchanged letters regularly with my parents. We tried to be positive. During my free time I turned to my Egyptology notebook, reading and fantasizing myself into another time.

About Enemies. Considering the situation and the apparent senselessness of it all, it was no surprise that some kids ran away. Given a chance we all would have done it. But run to where? There was no place to hide. The kids who ran away usually went home or tried to get to relatives or people they knew. Some of the latter, afraid for themselves, might turn them in. The *Heer* called it desertion and punished it with death. Military police or regular police were good at tracking deserters down and bringing them back to Sagan. There they were executed on the shooting range by a firing squad of their comrades. If there were trials we never heard about them.

The shooting range was a large complex, consisting of perhaps a dozen or more long shooting lanes separated by longitudinal, sod-covered walls. This was where we fired rifles, MG 42s, and *Sturmgewehre*. One day I saw an execution by accident. Our platoon had a cigarette break. I was putting up a new target in front of the roof-covered sandy backdrop at the end of the shooting lane. I heard voices across the side wall to my left. I crawled up and looked over.

There was a pole in front of the backdrop. A kid stood limp at the pole. A sergeant tied his hands around the pole behind him. The sergeant walked away to stand by a squad of riflemen, kids. He barked a command. Ten rifles fired and hit. The body was slammed against the pole, then fell forward. He was held by the rope, slumped head down. The sergeant stepped close, removed the prisoner's cap and shot him in the head with a pistol. I had seen enough. I slid back down the wall.

Life was cheap. Who was the enemy? Our own or those others pushing toward the Rhine from the west? We never learned how many kids were executed this way during or before our time in Sagan *Kaserne*, victims of our own military.

Two guys in my squad trusted me enough to tell me about their plans to run away, despite knowing what would happen if they got caught. Erich and Herbert, both from Neuss, great kids, bright, good-looking. "I know of a cabin near Schalksmühle," Erich said. "It's in the forest. No one lives there. It's a hunting cabin. I have been there with my father. "

"How far is it from here to the cabin?" I asked.

"I don't know. Maybe twenty kilometers."

We thought about it for a while. "How can we travel twenty kilometers?" I asked. "They will look for us at our homes. That would be all right. But everyone who sees us will know we are deserters. We can't trust anyone. They will call the police on us."

We sat in a heavy silence, dispirited. We talked about it a few more times. I could not get the execution I had seen out of my mind. I saw no chance for safely getting away. I talked them out of it. And so we didn't run. Erich was killed in battle in front of Kirchhellen. The last time I saw Herbert he was stumbling back from our foxholes, pressing a first-aid package to where his lower jaw had been ripped away by a .50 caliber machine-gun bullet.

My Parents and the Sergeant-Major. Late on the morning of February 23, our company was out on an exercise when a lance-corporal came from headquarters on a bicycle. He brought an order to return. When we arrived I saw my parents standing with the sergeant- major. He waved me over after the company was dismissed. It was near lunchtime. My parents embraced me. The sergeant-major invited them to have lunch with the troops in the mess hall. I was embarrassed at first, but happy to see them. My parents were the only parents who visited the base during our time there. I noticed that my father had put on the small medal clips of his decorations from WW I. The sergeant-major had recognized them. As a favor from one old soldier to another he had ordered the company back to base. It was most unusual. I wondered how our lieutenant felt about this matter. He had not objected. Whatever the reasons, my parents and I were together one more time.

We spent the afternoon in the empty mess hall. We talked but it was difficult. We didn't say what we really felt. I loved them but didn't tell them. I couldn't. I knew it was the same for them. We revealed ourselves only through little gestures. In some way I was remote, already belonging to something else. My father understood, my mother not so much. Still, there was a bond between us that was unbreakable.

Their train to Gerresheim left the Wuppertal-Elberfeld station around 6 P.M. I asked the sergeant-major if I could accompany my parents to the railway. He gave me leave. The way down the road was hard for us. We didn't talk much. At the station we stood together for a while. I left before their train arrived. I remember their hollow faces, huge eyes, the near desperation on my mother's face.

The sergeant-major had been wounded seven times. He was a most experienced soldier but a kind man. War had not hardened him. In fact, it had made him soft. He called us kids in his company his *Jungens*. He tried to be sort of a father for the fathers who could not be there, some already dead or lost in the war. He despised office work and let others run it. He talked to us often, trying to tell us what he had learned that we might live. He was to die among his *Jungens* on the road to Kirchhellen before the battle, struck down by an artillery shell. Of all the other men I met in positions of command in the *Heer*, none was remarkable. He was, and I remember him for it, just as I remember the *Jungens* who died there with him.

Moving Out. On March 3, American troops reached Oberkassel, the suburb of Düsseldorf across the river on the left bank of the Rhine. From that date on, the city lay under artillery fire. German troops had blown the four bridges that spanned the river to Neuss and Oberkassel. The radio reported that the government had declared Düsseldorf a fortress to be held at any cost. We could clearly hear the rumble of frequent bombardments. Had we been sent to the frontline there, we would have understood. After all, it would have made some sense. But it was not to be. Our training continued as if nothing else mattered, as if nothing had changed. Those of us in our battalion from Düsseldorf and Neuss fretted the most about our families, but we all were very much disturbed.

The continuing air war was remorseless. From March 2 to March 18, the RAF and the USAF bombed eleven cities in our neighborhood: Köln on March 2, Dortmund, 3-4, Dortmund and Siegen, on the 7th, Dortmund and Essen on the 8th, Essen on the 11th, Dortmund on the 10th and 12th, Hagen on the night of 15-16. Wuppertal-Elberfeld, although we thought there was nothing left to destroy, was not spared. The cities below us, below Sagan *Kaserne*, were nevertheless struck again on March 13, this time by the RAF in a daytime raid. We were on a training exercise away from the base. We saw the Lancasters in bright daylight following the Wupper River from the west and unloading over the cities. There were perhaps 80 to a hundred planes flying at a height of 4,000 meters (13,000 feet). We could actually see twelve large bombs drop from the bomb bay of each plane, hear the terrifying sound of their fall and the horrendous impact in the valley. Being on the plateau, we could not see the bombs strike, but we saw the columns of dust and debris rise into the air. The ground we were on literally shook under our feet. We did not take cover. We were not the target. We stood by, observers, frightened sheep.

Five days later, on March 18, our time finally came. Trucks lined up and the order to move was issued. Not for the protection of Düsseldorf and the Rhine but to an assignment elsewhere. We climbed aboard in battle gear. It was clear that our battalion would go into combat. We wondered where, but no one told us. We sat in uneasy silence. There was no escape. What was to come would come, whatever it would be.

At the head of the column of trucks was an open *Kübelwagen* with the battalion commander, a Major Klocke. We had seen him only a few times during training and he had made no impression on us. With him was a staff officer beside the driver, a lance-corporal. The company lieutenants and the sergeant-major rode with the grenadiers. We took a route in a northeastern direction, evading the large broken cities such as Hagen, Dortmund and Hamm. We took side roads through villages and small towns. We had left in fog but after we passed Dortmund the sky cleared. We had come into a region where Allied fighter-bombers dominated the sky. A couple of times we passed shot-up military vehicles on the road. Travel was slow. Anxious eyes watched the sky. Once, when the convoy had stopped in good cover, a flight of American Thunderbolts, noses painted bright red, swooped over, not more than 300 meters above ground. They attacked a train less than one kilometer away with bombs and cannon fire, leaving the locomotive and a couple of cars a burning mess. We watched with dread. Eventually we arrived safely in a village in eastern Westphalia, somewhere south of Münster. Our battalion was quartered in farmers' barns. We heard a rumor that an Allied airborne landing was expected east of the Ruhr. There were more troops billeted in villages around us.

On the Road. They kept us in readiness in the village but nothing happened. On March 19 the last mail was delivered to us. How the mail got through from Sagan to us was astounding. There was a last letter from my mother, dated March 12. A word-for-word translation reads like this: "My dear, dear *Junge*, I will write you quickly a few lines. The two of us here are all right. How is it with you? We have become used to living in the basement. It can be done. At least we are safe from artillery fire. How far is your training? We hope they don't throw you into the mess five minutes before the end. Be strong and don't lose your trust in God, my *Lieb*, then He will help and protect us. So often He has clearly helped us. So, my *Lieb*, God be with you. His blessings, and affectionate greetings from *Vati* and

Mutti. It is so hard for us that we cannot visit you. But it is impossible. The trains leave from Erkrath and we cannot get there. Adieu, my *Lieb*."

One evening, when I was on guard duty, a Yugoslav farm hand stopped and started a conversation. He told me where he came from, and that he had been working on one village farm for all his time as a prisoner of war. He asked me where I was from. I told him. He made a sad face. "Düsseldorf surrendered twelve days ago, didn't you know?" I said, "No, that can't be. Who told you?"

"The BBC reported it," he said.

I showed him the letter stamped March 12. So the BBC lied. Everybody lied. But why had American troops stopped their advance opposite Düsseldorf and not taken the city? Or had they by now? For my parents that would mean the war was over.

On March 25 the order came to move out. On a rainy day with low hanging clouds we walked west-southwest. We walked in full combat harnesses. We carried our individual rifle or *Sturmgewehr*, ammo, and hand grenades. Each of us also carried extra belts of rounds slung around the neck and metal boxes with ammo for the MG 42s. Every third or fourth kid also carried a *Panzerfaust*. We wore our canvas sheets as ponchos. Under the ponchos the gas mask box was on our back. To the belt were attached side arm, ammo pouches, a short spade, canvas food bag, and canvas-covered water bottle. We wore our ski cap-like hats and had our helmet attached to our food bag.

We walked in single file by squad. The MG gunner followed behind the squad leader. Behind the gunner came the guy with the reserve barrels for the MG along with his own weapon. 1st Company was in the lead, followed by 2nd and 3rd companies. We walked in a staggered formation, one squad on the left hand side of the road above the ditch, the next squad on the right hand side, and so on. We kept the road free for military vehicles going in both directions.

We were lucky that day. The bad weather prevented the fighter-bombers from flying sorties in our area. Once we stopped on the road to eat our rations. They consisted of the hard, dark bread baked for the military (*Kommiss-Brot*) and a sausage of unknown components we called *Timoshenko*. The word *Timoshenko* was meant as analogy, referring to a relationship between this Soviet general's known merciless exploitation of his soldier in battle and a sausage that might contain a component other than of animal origin. Anyway, the term was very widely used. We sat and cut slices of bread and covered them with *Timoshenko*.

We bivouaked for the night outside the town of Haltern, after a walk of 45 kilometers. We took quarters on farms where supplies reached us with hot food, and cold rations for the next days. All night long we heard sporadic artillery fire from the front to the west. Our squad corporal told us that American troops had crossed the Rhine north of Dinslaken on March 23, that the 116th Panzer Division had fought a tank battle with American armor and was slowly withdrawing east. He added that we were to reinforce the grenadiers of the 116th.

Moving In. In continuing bad weather the next morning we marched on Dorsten, eighteen kilometers to the southwest. There was quite a bit of traffic on the road, trucks, more trucks, a few self-propelled guns (Marder IIIs), and Red Cross cars. Getting closer to Dorsten we twice passed permanent anti-aircraft batteries, one of 10.5 caliber, the other, good old 8.8. We also saw *Heer* batteries of field guns under camouflage netting.

As we trudged on, once in a while one of our squads started singing, and their songs were picked up by other squads and platoons. Our songs were, "Ja, die Tochter der Navajo..." ("Yeah, the daughter of the Navajos... ") – not exactly a traditional German marching song. Or, "Auf der Heide blüht ein kleines Blümelein... " ("On the heath there blossoms a little flower... "). We sang out of defiance, I guess. Finally, the singing died away and we walked in silence.

What were we thinking? I don't remember. We had no illusions. We did not expect to come out alive unless something miraculous happened. One kid in the next squad, an ex-*Flakhelfer*, actually repeated the Latin text of the epigram the gladiators spoke after entering the arena, "Ave, Caesar, morituri te salutant" – "Greetings Caesar, those who are about to die salute you."

It revealed what was going on inside us. Before us was only an end, not a salvation. But we would do what we had learned, and we would release, violently, the turmoil, anger, and frustration penned up inside us.

We saw the smoking ruins of Dorsten from a distance. We learned that the RAF had attacked the city in a daytime raid on Wednesday, March 22, four days earlier. It had been one of many attacks on the medieval town, but this one destroyed what had been left. Hundreds of people were working in the rubble, perhaps trying to rescue some who were buried alive. We marched on in silence. All of us had witnessed similar scenes many times over. Still, this hardly served to endear to us the Allied soldiers we were certain to meet soon. An old man came out and wished us good luck. We asked about fighter-bombers. Yes, he said, they come almost every day, but two days earlier seven had been shot down by light Flak over Marl, a few kilometers to the southeast. Perhaps he exaggerated, but we were glad to hear it.

Farther on, within sight of Kirchhellen, a small town with tightly clustered houses around a church with a high steeple, we passed through a large, open area with fields on both sides of the road. When the leading platoon of our company was perhaps a kilometer away from the town, a low-flying American spotter plane appeared suddenly out of the dreary sky and circled over the battalion. A few of our MGs cut loose but the plane ducked and went away. Our sergeant-major ran between the platoons and shouted for us to hurry to the town. We ran, the other companies following. It did not take long until the first artillery shells exploded in the fields around us. Most by far burst there, but a few hit the road.

Coming under heavy artillery fire for the first time is one of the most haunting experiences of my life. Many years later, after leaving a girlfriend's house late one evening, I walked at the foot of a brush-covered slope as a party went on above. People must have started to light fireworks. I heard the unmistakable whine of a projectile coming down and threw myself in the dirt for cover. I was wearing my finest suit. As I lay there, I felt like a fool, but my brain had remembered.

That late morning before Kirchhellen is deeply embedded in my memory. We made it into town through the crashing salvoes of enemy shells. We left some of our dead and wounded on the road, our sergeant-major among them. While the barrage continued behind us we went through empty streets. I remember a dead lieutenant lying on his back, both forearms upright, as if reaching for heaven. Our major and two officers stood by the staff car and watched us pass. It was the last time I saw them. A little farther west of town, on a low rise, we dug in on fields on both sides of a road leading into Kirchhellen from the west, 1st Company in the center, 2nd Company to the left, 3rd Company to the right.

An eerie silence fell over us while we were digging. The spotter plane returned. Somewhere from the west of us came the rattle of a *Vierling* 2cm gun I knew so well. The plane made a quick dive and escaped. Artillery fire opened up on our position. We continued to dig furiously, two-man foxholes, while we were being pounded. Screams. Casualties. My buddy, Ulli, stronger than I, did most of the digging while I lay flat on the ground.

The shelling lasted perhaps half an hour before it stopped. Wounded were carried back. We looked around. From the holes of my platoon we could not see the positions of 3rd Company to the north, nor anything of 2nd Company to the south. They were hidden by patches of brush and trees, and in the south by a rise of ground. Two hundred meters west of us and a little to the left of our platoon was a small farmhouse. In the distance, perhaps 400 meters away, lay the empty revetments of a heavy Flak battery that had been withdrawn a week before.

Behind the revetments were a few widely spaced farm buildings. By the road to the right of us sat a disabled *Panther* tank, one of its tracks blown.

From the farms in the distance we heard the familiar sawing sounds of an MG 42. Silence again. After a while a squad of grenadiers walked casually across the field in single file, passed through south of us, and vanished. Once more the rattle of the *Vierling*. The sound of tank tracks. A *Wirbelwind* (a *Vierling* mounted on a Panzer IV chassis) emerged in the distance and rolled toward us. It swung by the two-man holes of our platoon and stopped. The tank carried on the front the *Windhund* (Greyhound) markings of the 116th Panzer Division. A few of us walked up to it. Veteran soldiers in heavy overcoats manned the tank. We stood together and lit cigarettes. I looked at the men with envy. How I would have loved to be the gunner on that tank. We talked a little. They mounted and raised their hands and rolled away. Now we were the frontline.

Afternoon, Evening. Nothing happened for a while. We heard the rumble of artillery fire to the north and south of us, but nothing was directed against us. In late afternoon a sergeant saw through binoculars some movement around the Flak revetments and the farms beyond. Perhaps he reported it by radio or a German artillery observer spied it from the Kirchhellen church tower. German artillery let loose and pounded the revetments and the farms. We thought the fire was pretty accurate. It lasted for perhaps ten minutes and left the farmhouses in flames. No further movement was seen for a while. But from the shelter of the revetments a couple of .50 caliber machine-guns sent streams of bullets into our position. I was afraid they might be mounted on Sherman tanks. Tanks were our major fear. We sat in our foxholes and endured the punishment. Ulli chewed a piece of bread from our rations. I was too tense to eat.

After a while the machine-gun fire died down. Perhaps they had run out of ammunition. We spied over the rim of our hole. We saw nothing. Dark came. We sat on the bottom of the pit. And then a single rifle shot came from our right. We stood up and looked. We saw many tiny figures running toward us at an angle in front of the burning farms. We could clearly see the men against the fires behind them. Flares went up. All along our line MGs hammered and rifles cracked. Because of the distance our rifles probably did little damage if any, but the MGs did. And then our artillery got into it and sent a barrage in to the attack. The assault faltered quickly.

We were grim, tired, mentally stressed. We felt no satisfaction. Some of those on the other side had died and been wounded. None of us had been hurt during the last 30 minutes. But this was not over yet. This would go on.

Second Day. We dozed the night away in our holes. Artillery exchanges took place to the south and north of us. Before our line everything was quiet. We never saw our company lieutenant. Was he dead, or where was he? We would have liked a friendly word, something reassuring. First light came and we noticed that the field by the revetments in front of the smoldering farms had been cleared of bodies. The ground was cratered but empty. Where was the enemy?

Around midday we suddenly heard the terrible sound of tank tracks to the west and northwest, grinding motors. Hulks of Sherman tanks, colored olive drab, came on the road and over the open field to our right. Many. What should we do? The Shermans rolled on. An explosion close by. The *Panther* we had believed finished had swung its turret and started to shoot with his big gun. The first Sherman blew up with a tremendous explosion. More Shermans shook violently from the impact of armor piercing shells. They hit with a loud clang. We watched as the *Panther* shot up a dozen Shermans and the rest pulled back. We were jubilant. Burning tanks everywhere. Ammunition exploded. German artillery hit the road and the farms again.

Quiet once more. Then an angry barrage of artillery fire enveloped our line. Some of the foxholes of our company were caved in or blew up with direct hits. Screams of wounded. Ulli and I sat against the wall of the foxhole, wishing we could crawl into the earth. A nightmare. There was no escape from it. Finally we looked at each other. Pale faces. Our dead were left in their foxholes. The wounded were carried back to Kirchhellen on stretchers made of ponchos. We never saw a medic.

Our numbers had shrunk. But there was not another attack. We had no communication with the companies to the left and right of us. We only saw and watched the ground directly in front of us up to the farms in the distance. No movement there. No one came and talked to us until that evening. The sergeant of third platoon came by our foxholes. He thought the companies had withdrawn to Kirchhellen. Those from our company who had carried the wounded or helped the walking wounded had not come back. He thought they had been held and added to a new defensive line farther back. He said we would remain where we were until orders came to pull back. We waited.

The night passed. We were uncertain. We didn't know what to think. We spent an uneasy night. A bad smell still came from two Shermans brewed up closest. It started to rain. We were soaked in our wet pits. Rain covers everything, washes everything, cleans. Or does it?

Third Day. Morning came, a grey misty day, March 28. We saw no movement across the fields to the right of us or before us. To the south, on our left, we couldn't see farther than about 70 meters. 2nd Company was supposed to be there. Were the few of us being surrounded? We were jittery. We waited in an eerie silence as if war held its breath. I looked at the farmhouse close to us. There was a gaping hole in the roof from an artillery shell. I saw a movement in the rafters and brought my carbine up, fired a couple of quick shots, and sat down. Ulli looked at me curiously.

Why? Why a couple of shots? An impulse? A response to the unnerving quiet? What reason was there?

No answering shots. Silence. A voice. "Come on out! Come on out!" Someone came toward us, repeating, "Come on out!" We looked over the rim of our hole. An American soldier in khaki, holding his rifle in the crook of his left arm. He walked straight up toward us. "What do we do?" someone called from a foxhole to my right. No one answered. No word from the sergeant. The American soldier did not dodge or weave. Two MGs and our rifles were trained on him. He kept coming, shouting, waving his free right hand. So we didn't shoot him. It would have been murder. He walked up to Ulli's and my foxhole. I guess we were the closest. He looked down at us from where he stood. "Come on out." His face was that of an American Indian, a face I had seen in some of my books. It had all the physical features.

I climbed out of the hole, Ulli following. He took my helmet off and threw it down. "Drop it," he said to the others who were getting out too. When I tried to reach down to grab my canvas bag to retrieve my Egyptology notebook, he held me by the arm and said, "Let's go. Put your hands on your heads," or something like that. So I lost that notebook but perhaps gained my life. He turned and walked away without looking back. We followed him. We walked around the bullet-scarred farmhouse into the farmer's inner court.

One M 3 Stuart light tank stood in a corner. It had probably slipped in during the night. There were about 30 to 40 soldiers. Some pushed us against the wall of the house. Ulli was on the far left end, I next to him. Willi and Helmut were to my right. I guess we were seventeen in all, the sergeant at the end to the right. He had been the last to come. Soldiers came forward and took our watches, rifling our pockets. In my left breast pocket I had Sherriff's play, *Journey's End*, in the right pocket my diary. The soldier who checked me took the English play but gave me back my diary. He looked at my tobacco pipe and gave it back, too. I didn't see the Indian soldier who had brought us in.

A bright flash. Our sergeant still had the flare gun on his belt. A soldier had taken it and fired it into a trench the farmer had built as a shelter. The flare exploded and bounced out, burning harmlessly. The soldiers around us hit the ground. We kept standing, too tired to react, too worn from what had happened, what was happening.

A sergeant among the soldiers became enraged. He grabbed a BAR from one of his men. He pushed our sergeant with the muzzle of the gun toward the farmer's dung heap a few meters away. He shot our sergeant in the back. The sounds of bullets hitting flesh. He came for the next one. I only saw the first two executions. I looked into the faces of the soldiers in front of me. Clouded, troubled faces, but no one protested or interfered.

What does one think in this situation? Nothing. The world becomes a blank, an empty slate. Nothing matters anymore.

Suddenly a jeep. An officer shouted. Stopped it. Four of us were left. We were made to run behind the jeep over the torn fields. The officer drove. Two soldiers had gotten into the back of the jeep and covered us with their rifles. We must have been very dangerous kids. German artillery shells exploded around us. We got to a farmhouse and were taken to a barn. Six more German prisoners were there, none from our battalion. I asked one of the two soldiers who had brought us – both wore the Combat Infantry Badge on their chests. "Why did he kill?" The man shrugged. "You killed two of his old buddies yesterday."

So. On the Sagan shooting range and before Kirchhellen a seventeen year old in a German uniform was worth only a few bullets.

We sat in the barn, prisoners of war. Alive. Alive, when so many others on both sides were not. Without the Indian stepping in, I was sure that I would have died in the foxhole. This unknown Indian soldier, one like the old-time warriors in the books I had read, was one of the bravest men I ever met. Yes. I owed him.

7

POW

March 28-September 24 1945

On the Road. No more prisoners joined the four of us. After two hours a truck came and took us away. Again, two soldiers kept their rifles trained on us. On the road to Wesel, twenty kilometers to the northwest, we went by such an accumulation of material and equipment that it shocked us: ammunition and gasoline dumps along the road in the open, vehicles of many kinds in a profusion beyond our imagination from jeeps through various types of trucks to armored personnel carriers and tanks, mostly Shermans. Batteries of different caliber guns, supply depots. They had it all. They had it in such amount that it was demented for Germany to continue fighting against this. And soldiers – where we had a hundred they had five times that number, or more. For every tank of ours they had fifty. What did it matter if ours were better? For each shell that reached our batteries after running the gauntlet of their fighter-bombers and the carpet bombing of their big planes, they had a thousand at their disposal. They did not have to fear air attacks from our side. The *Luftwaffe* was no longer a viable force. Their supplies were endless.

But despite their colossal superiority in numbers we still made them bleed. We saw first aid stations and field hospitals, Red Cross vehicles going our way or going in the opposite direction. In the fields we also saw the burned-out hulks of Shermans and a few of ours, three *Panthers* and one *StuG III*. A cratered landscape, broken farms, wrecked villages. We also saw the first black American soldiers; they were driving trucks and working in kitchens and supply areas. Later we learned the American brass did not trust blacks in combat.

Now we were onlookers, not targets anymore. We saw no German civilians. Where were they? What happened to them? We were taken to a collection point on a farm where we were joined by about 30 German POWs of all ages, from kids like us to veteran soldiers. There were none from our battalion. We asked. A few were lightly wounded, with blood-soaked bandages. From there we were trucked farther west in the afternoon, crossing the Rhine on a pontoon bridge near the former Wesel stone bridge. The great bridge had been blown, its middle part now an obstacle in the river where debris and some bodies had accumulated. The bridgehead on the east bank, where the US 82nd Airborne Division had forced a foothold a week ago, still showed the wreckage of battle.

Our truck took us to a wide meadow on the west bank where perhaps 500 German prisoners were confined to a narrow space within a parameter marked with a red rope. Machine-guns were posted on two sides. What were the Americans afraid of? A riot? We were glad to have the war behind us.

We sat or stood densely packed. We were given neither food nor water. Water we needed most. I was dehydrated. Once, when an American soldier walked by, I asked if I could go to the river for some water. He looked at me curiously but made a sign that I could go. I slipped under the rope and walked to the river's edge, about a hundred meters away. I drank deeply.

It was a very bad mistake. Father Rhine gave me a terrible dysentery. It combined with jaundice, and the two together almost killed me. It took me many weeks in the POW camp to recover.

Rennes. We spent two miserable days by the Rhine without food, water and shelter. On the morning of the third day black soldiers trucked us to the Belgian city of Namur, about 200 kilometers to the southwest. On a wide open square we climbed from the trucks and were marched to the railway station. We had been expected. We passed through a crowd of enraged citizens that showered us with insults and thrown objects, from soft eggs to stones. Our guards had an interesting time watching our misery. They couldn't have stopped it if they had wanted to. We marched in ranks, the wounded in the middle. No command was given, but we marched in step to show our disregard, our defiance to this humiliation. We stared straight ahead, ignoring insults and missiles as if they did not concern us. All of us had experienced worse. The entire world had become our enemy. We made the station with more injured than we started with, and were packed like sardines into closed cattle cars. Each car had one bucket to urinate and defecate in, and one bucket with drinking water. We were starved on the slow, long haul to a POW camp near Rennes in Brittany, France.

On the train my dysentery and jaundice came into full bloom. I was wet and weak and stank like hell. My three buddies, the other survivors of the Kirchhellen shootings, formed a protective cordon around me. I lay helpless on the floor in a corner below the slit of a window. There was a murmur among bystanders that I should be thrown from the train if that was possible. I could not hold down the water my buddies gave me. My empty bowels ejected blood.

I do not remember how long the train ride lasted. Part of the time I was unconscious. The doors opened from the outside. Soldiers shouted, "Mack snell! Mack snell!" We lumbered out and were pushed to form up and hurry. I remember that I was more lifted than dragged by two of my buddies. I had my arms around their necks. I couldn't walk. We made it to a place where we got hot food, the first meal in days. It was a red vegetable soup, dipped into empty tomato cans from a trash barrel that had been transformed into a soup pail. We stood in line. Each of us got a full ladle. The four of us sat together. I could not eat. I gave my portion to my buddies. The soldier at the soup pail, the master of the food, called out. Something was left. My buddies encouraged me to get a refill. They helped me up and moved me toward the pail. A crowd had gathered. The pail master pointed at me and called for me to come forward. I looked behind me. I didn't understand that it was me he wanted. But my buddies shoved me on. So I was the first. I didn't know how pitiful I looked. For four or five days or more I had not only eaten nothing but lost everything short of my intestines. A few days later I was weighed. The scale said, 95 pounds. I must have lost about 40 pounds. Surprise.

This was our welcome to the POW camp near Rennes. We were registered and given American Army blankets. They quartered us in large tents, each POW with about one meter in space in a row on the barren ground. It was a rectangular space, counted from the tent wall to the walkway through the center of the tent. Prisoners lay on both sides of it. For a cushion I had a brick with a GI cap on top to rest my head on. Important objects were one can for coffee and one can for soup. Each POW regarded his array of empty cans as his personal property.

The Rennes camp was a well-established camp when we arrived. Two food items were plentiful: coffee and lemon juice water, the latter available all day long in canvas bags on stands spread around the camp. We lined up for food twice a day: at 5 A.M. and 5 P.M. Each time we got a watery vegetable soup and coffee, good coffee. At the 5 P.M. food serving, each of us, in addition to the soup, got one slice of soft white bread (one loaf for twelve men). These were starvation rations. Although no one died of hunger, hardly anyone was nursed back to health either.

There was no hospital for our treatment. A group of German doctors, POWs themselves, were housed in a tent in camp and did what they could. I was helped to see them. I was weighed and examined. The physician who checked me diagnosed that I had dysentery and jaundice. He had no medicines whatsoever. He suggested that I should eat coffee grounds. I did. But it took a long time, it seemed, until I could eat normally.

As the Holocaust came to Rennes. Five weeks after our arrival the war ended with Germany's capitulation. A newspaper in German was handed out in camps with information on Hitler's suicide. There was more news. Pages and pages of photographs taken by Allied photographers in such liberated concentration camps as Bergen-Belsen, Dachau, and others that showed mounds of nude, emaciated dead bodies.

We looked at these pictures and said, no, that can't be. That can't be true. This is Allied propaganda. We looked again and again. Eventually we understood: these pictures must be true. This could not be staged. Finally the full horror of the Nazis revealed itself to us. What was also revealed was that we had been suckers, fighting a war while, behind our backs and in secret, the SS slaughtered innocent men, women and children by the hundreds of thousands, even millions, as we learned later.

We were shocked, dumbfounded, depressed. I had known since I was six years old that there had been concentration camps. That they had become death camps where people were systematically murdered was something we had not known. We were so ignorant that sometimes we even thought that being an inmate in a concentration camp might not be so bad. Inmates didn't have to become soldiers and get killed or crippled like so many of us on the outside. We finally realized how badly we had been betrayed.

What the Allies had done by bombing cities and killing civilians in great numbers had been bad enough. It stiffened our resistance. Sometimes it seemed there was a reason to fight on because the Allies were determined to destroy everything German, to wipe out German culture once and for all.

But now we saw that it had been our people, the Nazis more than the Allies, who were the destroyers of Germany. Looking at the pictures we said, "They will never let us go. They will work us in their mines and camps until we are dead." We were a depressed bunch in that huge prison camp. What did it matter that we had fought honorably, we thought, for our homeland ravaged by vicious bombing. At least we *Flakhelfer* had thought that. But we were Germans. After the Bergen-Belsens, even though we had not known about them, we were all considered criminals.

We witnessed individual acts of cruelty from some of the American guards. They were fresh from the US and had not been in combat with German troops. They, too, had seen the concentration camp pictures and read about it. They must have thought that we, behind the barbed wire, and at their mercy, had been complicit in mass murder. I saw a guard flip a lit cigarette from the watch tower down to the interior wire, then shooting dead the POW who went to get the cigarette he thought the guard wanted him to have. Or a guard shooting a POW during the night, under blazing lights, as the POW walked to the latrine. Sometimes, during the night, a guard, probably bored, shot rounds into our tents. Some POWs were wounded that way. We were only Germans. We heard that General Eisenhower, Supreme Commander of Allied forces in Europe, said after Bergen-Belsen, "The only good German soldier is a dead German soldier." We were the new Indians, I thought. Never mind that the SS had committed the murders without the German public's knowledge. Those who had known kept silent, fearing for their own lives.

In May a ragged new bunch of POWs was added to our camp. These were survivors of Bad Kreuznach, one of the many American camps for German POWs hastily put together after the German surrender. They told horror stories. They knew of dozens of such camps along the Rhine and farther west. In these, POWs died by the thousands. It seemed that American officials in charge of POW camps took the Supreme Commander's verdict to heart.

But our POW camp at Rennes was not a death camp. American authorities let us starve a little, and sometimes a POW was shot for no reason. Bad enough, but that was all. In late June all POWs under eighteen were called up and marched to the railway station for transfer. Where, we were not told. We feared that we might be shipped to coal mines somewhere or to some other nasty place. My three buddies and I were part of the "Children's Exodus."

Once in the Rennes camp we had gotten tobacco: two red cans of Prince Albert tobacco for each POW along with paper to roll cigarettes. I still had my pipe. I enjoyed the Virginia leaf tobacco tremendously. It seemed a gift from another world. The red cans of Prince Albert I have always remembered warmly.

Train to Ste. Mère-Eglise. We were allowed our customary vegetable soup and coffee at 5 A.M. before we marched. We got no rations for the journey. The train was long, consisting of open cars that had been used for transporting coal. The cars, therefore, were full of coal dust. In each car was one bucket for lavatory use and one with water. We were told that we were not to leave a car without a guard's permission; if a POW did he would be shot. The train passed slowly through the Brittany countryside in a north to northeast direction. It seemed we would go to Normandy. Why?

People gathered on some railroad bridges near villages or small towns, shouting insults and throwing objects into our open cars, anything that was at hand, usually stones, but I also saw an old bicycle frame lifted and thrown. We had no protection against it. A couple of kids were injured from bricks. Our guards saw it all but did nothing. We gathered the smaller stones thrown and, after a while, waited for the next bridge. When people there started throwing objects we threw stones in return. That sometimes ended it.

In the afternoon we reached St. Lô at the bottom of the Cherbourg Peninsula. The city had seen some hard fighting after the Allied landings in June 1944. Allied bombers and house-to-house fighting had wrecked the city as badly as Essen, Düsseldorf, Köln, Duisburg, Wuppertal, etc. The train came to a stop at the main railway station. Many people stood on the platform waiting for trains. But no insults were hurled at us here; the people stood quietly.

Something happened there I will always remember. A lone Frenchman in his thirties ran along our train from car to car and took empty water buckets and rushed to fill them. He worked to supply as many cars with fresh water as he could before the train pulled out. He had been a prisoner of war in Germany and spoke our language well. Apparently he had had good experiences. This one man was, to me, a bolt of lightning in the darkness.

The train turned north toward Cherbourg. This confirmed our worst fears. They will ship us from Cherbourg harbor, some said. They will never let us go home. Home, where was that? Did home still exist? Our parents and others we knew, were they still alive? Those whose homeland was in East Prussia or other areas overrun by the Russians, did their loved ones still live? Had they been displaced, were they on roads somewhere, or had they disappeared in the great killing frenzy?

As the train trundled on, one by one the guys in my car lay down to sleep. We were weak, underfed, and emotionally exhausted. But I could not sleep. As the night came on I stood at the sidewall of the car, my elbows on the wooden rim, my chin in my hands, staring into the dark. The train pulled into Carentan, another damaged city, and stopped. A well-lit passenger train drew up on the track next to us. A window was directly in front of me. If I had stretched out my arm I could almost have touched it. The window was rolled down and four young people peered out, two French soldiers in immaculate uniforms and their girl friends. These four were pretty and full of life, well-dressed, clean, laughing happily. Their faces and mine were on the same level. I kept staring, looking through them, through these happy faces. They looked at me and then into the car where my guys lay bundled up in the black dust, looking dead. Their smiles faded from their faces. They became sober, serious, perhaps even worried. I neither changed my position nor my stare. I meant them no harm. These four had done nothing bad to us. They were not enemies, just strangers who had suddenly, without preparation, been confronted with a train that appeared as a train of the damned. And damned we were. The four became very still. And then their train left. As I remember this incident they probably remember it too. Perhaps they thought I was the last one alive. It looked that way. I rather saw myself as a guard, a watcher over my slumped buddies on the road to perdition.

St. Foucarville. When the train rolled into St. Mère-Eglise it halted for the last time. Shouts. Shouts. "Get out! Mack snell! Mack snell!" – familiar sounds. We had barely climbed out when we were driven like sheep. "Snell! Snell!" In the dark, under the headlights of trucks, we were forced to run on a narrow road. We staggered for six long kilometers. Many, many collapsed on that road and were thrown by soldiers into the trucks like sacks of garbage. I remember the clanking sound when someone fell, the empty cans of his "dinner ware" making a din. Eleven kids died that night we heard, perhaps more. Ulli of my old buddies, a kid of great strength, helped me to stay afoot and on the road. There were jeeps and more soldiers when we reached the POW camp of St. Foucarville. We were pushed into a prepared "cage" among a row of cages already filled. Each held 2,000 kids. That night all of us lay as still as the dead, like the ones who actually had died. The war was supposedly over, or was it? Later we learned that the guards who picked us up in Ste. Mère-Eglise had been told we were members of the SS Panzer Division *Hitlerjugend.*

The St. Foucarville POW camp consisted of two camps. One was an officers' camp, the other was a camp for us youngsters. Both camps were separated within the larger camp. The officers' camp housed a few thousand German officers, from generals to lieutenants. Our camp housed perhaps 50,000 kids or more in barbed wire cages (that is what they were called by our American guards), 2,000 to each cage. Each was separated by barbed wire from the next. Cages were located in two rows on both sides of the camp's main street. Both the officers' camp and our camp were enclosed with double rows of barbed wire and spaced guard towers. Some of the kids in our camp were *Flakhelfer* barely sixteen years old who had been captured in western Germany and brought in by train. We wondered why we had been concentrated there. What was the purpose of it? We still believed that "they," the "others," had planned something sinister, something special for us, something like shipment overseas for slave labor.

The camp was two kilometers off the coast, near Utah Beach, one of the beaches where American troops had forced a landing during the Normandy invasion. All day long we heard explosions as either mines were detonated or wrecked ships or landing craft were blown up. Once, on a work detail, a guard took six of us to Utah Beach. He had not yet seen it himself, so we saw it with him. He had not been in combat so what he saw meant little to him. Bullet-scarred bunkers, many wrecked ships run aground during the battle, others with hulls sticking out of the waves. It all contrasted sharply with the wide sweep of the ocean, so peaceful now.

On my second and last work detail we had some chores to do in the officers' camp. We met Hans-Ulrich Rudel there, the famous Stuka pilot who, with his "tank busting" Ju 87G, armed with two 3.7cm guns, had scored more than 500 Russian tank "kills". We sat with him and looked at the highest decorated German soldier of the war. He had been shot down a number of times and lost his right foot in one crash. Fitted with a prosthesis he had flown against the Russians to the last day of the war. The Americans had confiscated the prosthesis along with his medals. He was pleased to be with us, he said. He was a friendly man. He certainly was a German nationalist, but a soldier, not a Nazi hack.

It seemed that authorities in charge of POW camps followed the same routine everywhere. We were still fed as at Rennes, first at 5 A.M., then at 5 P.M. The amount of food and its consistency was the same as in Rennes. One could live on it. Barely.

Summer on Cherbourg Peninsula. It was a warm and pleasant summer on the peninsula. The weather was good, we had a lot of sun. I used the time to read a lot while sitting outside the tent in the sun. I was able to get some second- or third-hand American paperbacks, a few very good ones, among them a book by William Faulkner and one by Raymond Chandler. The Faulkner was hard to read. Much of it I didn't get, certainly not without a dictionary. I no longer made entrances in my diary after becoming a POW. Instead, I wrote poetry. I had the stump of a pencil left. Poetry does not take up much space, and space in my diary was limited. I also had lots of time to think. My eighteenth birthday came on July 31, and went.

I wondered how all of this had happened. The Nazis, of course. But why had so many people gone along with them? Why had German generals sent men into battle when they knew the war was lost, and by perpetuating it, they squandered so many lives and so much more? Why the desperate fighting to the end? Was this a German thing? What was German in that? And what should I do with that knowledge now? How could things be changed if we were given a chance? Should we be given that chance, I promised myself, I would work for change, for truth. I would never again be on the side of injustice. I thought often about my grandfather. He had been in this fight all his life.

Once, when our cage was marched somewhere, I don't remember the reason, black guards told us to sing a song. This had been our procedure: someone, an officer or whoever, called, "Ein Lied!" The right front man in the column called the song, "Heidemarie!" Then he called out, "Three, four!" The whole column started to sing after "Four," soldiers marching in step. That's what happened on the march when the soldier suggested a song. The right front man called the song. Our column, 2,000 kids, fell into step and we sang, "Wo König Ortler seinen Speer steil in die Lüfte…" Our singing reverberated through the whole camp. Everywhere kids and officers ran to the barbed wire fences to see what was happening. Not much. We blared our German marching song in the face of the world. For a few moments, we were POWs no more, a unit again. Perhaps, ready to fight once more?

The exercise, harmless as it was, must have scared the camp commander. Perhaps he realized that our spirit was on the mend. It never happened again that German soldiers (from fifteen to seventeen years of age) were encouraged to "sing a song."

After the initial cruelty that occurred upon our arrival I saw no acts of violence against us and did not hear of any. St. Foucarville was not a bad camp. Around the middle of September 1945, we were questioned about where we came from in Germany. It seemed we were going to be sent home! Home? Incredible. Nothing was done for those who came from regions no longer part of Germany, as for instance, East Prussia, Silesia, and areas east of the Oder River or under the control of Russians, Poles, Czechs, etc.

Those of us who were from the "British Zone of Occupation" in western and north-western Germany got orders that would take us by train to Weeze, a military camp southwest of Wesel. We could not believe it. But we were assembled, there was really a train, and it really took us away south and east. We were going home! We were going home after all.

Once again we rolled through "enemy territory," but this time there were no angry people to threaten us. What had happened? We came to the Weeze camp. Barbed wire still, but a different attitude among the English officers and men. With the place under English control, for once things were fair and reasonable.

We were de-loused and given good meals, the best we had had since we became POWs. We received discharge papers to the British Zone of Occupation, a 20 Mark bill to pay streetcar or train fare, and were released in small groups over a period of a couple of days. Free. Unbelievable. Actually free!

Düsseldorf. The Way Home. Outside the gate I suddenly stood all by myself. The others who had left with me had rushed in different directions. For a long time I had been in the constant company of many others, now I was alone. It was unnerving. I missed my buddies. They had kept me alive when I was deathly sick. Where were they? I pulled myself together. I slowly set my feet.

In the camps we had very much looked alike. Our German uniforms had long ago worn out. We had been clothed in surplus American khaki uniforms or hand-me-downs, stamped with the POW sign on backs and jackets. Our underwear had long perished also, so we wore yellow T-shirts and white cotton shorts. I had acquired a small canvas bag with a shoulder strap, US military equipment. Walking toward the streetcar stop I felt like a canary, like an outsider, a stranger among civilians who were supposedly my people. They looked me over briefly and knew immediately: I was a POW coming home, as in *Draussen vor der Tür*, an important radio play by Wolfgang Borchert of the period. People were extremely friendly and tried to be helpful. But I wasn't used to this. I had not seen regular people, civilians, for a long time. I was a stranger used to places and people they knew nothing about. It wasn't their fault, but I felt as estranged as someone coming from another planet. Was this Germany? I saw the ruins, all right. I had seen them before. I had seen them in St. Lô, too.

I made it by streetcar from Krefeld to Oberkassel, on the left bank of the Rhine opposite Düsseldorf. The bridges were still blown and the only way to cross was by boat. There was a line half a kilometer long, people waiting patiently for the one white-painted boat of the Köln-Düsseldorf Line that was going back and forth. I walked to the end of the line but people waved me on. As I walked along the line, people kept waving me on. One of the lost sons coming back.

I moved to the head of the line feeling dizzy. Why were all these civilians, older men, women, so friendly? What had I done? I stood as if I were a foreigner thrown into another culture. What did I have in common with them? I didn't know anymore. Was my home St. Foucarville and my buddies, the food lines at 5 A.M. and 5 P.M., nights on a small blanket covering my space on the ground, my head on a brick?

The boat came and everyone made space for me. They had been through hell and more. Was I somebody special? I did not think so. But that was what happened. The boat crossed and docked on the Düsseldorf side. I was let off first. I walked along the long line of people waiting to cross to the other side, feeling like a freak, like a copy of an American. Everyone looked at my American clothes and at my hollow, stony face.

The "alte Schlossturm," the castle keep on the Rhine, one of the city's landmarks overlooking the river, had been destroyed. So was most of the Old Town behind it. Of the large buildings along the river front most were burned out. Where were my parents? What should I prepare myself for? Streetcar no. 3 to Gerresheim had its end station near the ruin of the Schlossturm. A lot of people waited there. I went over and ran into a guy I knew, Manny Wilke, a guy my age from Gerresheim, a future soccer star. He made a ruckus, greeting me. I shrank back. I was not used to expressing emotions. As soon as I had a chance to speak I asked, "The villa, next to the Krone, is it still standing?" His answer was, yes. "Was the house hit?" No, he said, it wasn't.

I did not know what else to ask. Our house undamaged meant my parents should be alive! The tram came and we got on, again people letting me go first. I watched passively as the tram rolled through the rubble of the devastated heart of the city. Only on Grafenberger Allee and in Grafenberg, among the demolished houses were others, often bullet-scarred but intact. Manny was talking without pause but I didn't listen. I was distant. I don't remember what was going on in my head. I know I felt out of place. Here was the moment I had imagined so often in the camps – with fear, with hope, and knowing if it happened, how crucial it would be for me. It would decide my life. If my parents were dead I knew I would not want to live.

The long climb of the streetcar through the woods to the Hardt, then the slow descent down into upper Gerresheim. Blackened skeletons of buildings here and there, not too many. The center of the Old Town was bombed out. Then came Schönau-Strasse, from where I had left for Sagan *Kaserne* it seemed half a life ago. Finally, the streetcar stop near our house on Dörpfeld-Strasse. I got out and walked. I don't remember how I felt. Not joy, I was still estranged. I went through the gate to the house. I passed the big trees, including the one my father had marked before I left.

Someone had seen me from the window. A strange man in khaki coming toward the house. It was my aunt Lisbeth who gave the alarm. As I went up the stairs and rang the bell, my mother was already rushing down the stairs to open the heavy iron door. My mother's eyes were wide. "*Jung*!" She fell into my arms. We stood for a while. I followed her upstairs like a sleepwalker. My aunt, a heavy-set woman was there and hugged me hard. I wanted to get away from the commotion but I couldn't. I sat in the living room. It was not the way I remembered it. It was the first time I had been in a normal house for a long time. My mother told me that my father would soon be back from the factory, but she would have to tell him carefully that I was home. He was ill; his heart was weak and he had developed asthma.

She told me that he often stopped returning soldiers on the street and asked if they knew me, if they had seen me. I had been reported as "missing in action."

I looked out the window. Outside familiar trees, in the distance the cluster of old trees around the decayed observation tower, the *Ruine*. My old hunting ground.

Then my father came. My mother caught him on the stairs, informed him. He came through the door, breathing with difficulty. My mother was as I remembered her, but my father looked haggard and aged. Our eyes locked. We put our arms around each other. And so we stood. Yes, they were alive. I was alive. I was home.

Epilogue

Egyptology was not to become my profession although I always remembered how my reading about the mysteries of the Old and New Kingdom helped to protect my sanity. Instead I became an anthropologist.

But that came later. Back in Düsseldorf, from September 1945 to March 1946, I worked downtown on a team cleaning Bismarck-Strasse from the main railway station to Blumen-Strasse of mountains of rubble and debris. When school started again in April 1946, I returned to my old school, now under new leadership and a new name, Jacobi *Gymnasium*. We ex-*Flakhelfer* and ex-soldiers had to take a special two-year set of courses to make up for our lost time and lack of knowledge. We received the *Abitur*, the diploma that allowed us to attend a university, after a three-day exam in April 1948.

German universities, many damaged by bombing, restarted also in 1946. Due to sparse facilities and a shortage of professors, enrollment was limited to older students returning from POW camps and injured veterans. As anti-Nazi professors who had escaped the Holocaust returned to Germany, the universities regained new life. I enrolled at Bonn University for the Winter Semester 1949.

At Bonn I started with courses in German literature and Classical archaeology. Soon I switched to a double major in anthropology and the history of art. My Ph. D. dissertation was on the pre-Inca Nazca culture of the south coast of Peru (published in *Annali Lateranensi*, Monograph 23, Rome 1959). Perhaps my grandmother's stories about Inca treasures worked subconsciously on my mind. After the Ph.D. I worked in the Bonn Anthropology Department as a research assistant until I was awarded a post-doctoral Fellowship in anthropology at the University of Chicago in the summer of 1958.

At Chicago, I was strongly influenced by Sol Tax, who became my main professor and mentor. I had arrived at the end of the Fox Project, a ten-year program by Sol Tax and his graduate students with the Fox Indians in Iowa. During this program the principles of action anthropology were initiated, a new way of applying anthropological knowledge for the benefit of a host population. In 1969, when I was at Wichita State University in Kansas, I started a program with the Cheyenne in Oklahoma based on what was learned in the Fox Project.

After a brief return to Germany, where I worked at the University of Freiburg, I was invited, in 1962, by the University of Wichita (later Wichita State) to join the faculty as an anthropology professor. My wife and I went. We remained at the university for 30 years until I became Professor Emeritus in 1992.

During these years I have written six books and published 56 essays and articles in the scholarly journals of ten countries. I have been to Peru for my studies and have done fieldwork in the French Pyrenees, on the Arctic slopes of northern Alaska, on the Columbian Plateau, and through much of the Plains. I have served as a jury member on the Fourth Russell Tribunal, "The Rights of the Indians of the Americas," Rotterdam 1980. I served as an expert witness on two Cheyenne cases in Federal Court in Oklahoma City. I was guest professor in Germany twice, at the University of Göttingen and the University of Münster.

All my publications focus on American Indians. This book is the first one that steps outside that tradition. I wrote it as an old man, one of the still living survivors of the 1926-1927 generation of Germans that is called the "silent generation." We were silent because the horror we lived through paled against the horror of the Holocaust. I have broken my silence now. I hope that it measures as a contribution to understanding a time gone but not forgotten.

Afterword

Dr. John M. Janzen, Professor of Anthropology, Department of Anthropology, University of Kansas, Lawrence, Kansas

Flakhelfer to Grenadier is a highly personal account of a now old man who was drafted by the German army at the end of World War II. Karl Schlesier is a well-known anthropologist in the United States, living in retirement in New Mexico where he has continued his scholarly career. His best known works include *Wolves of Heaven: Cheyenne Shamanism, Ceremonies and Prehistoric Origins* 1985, and his edited volume *Plains Indians, AD 500-1500: The Archeological past of Historic Groups* 1994. Most recently he has published a trilogy of carefully-researched historical novels on American Indian groups that resisted containment by the United States in the late 19th century: *Trail of the Red Butterfly* is about a Plains Indian expedition into Mexico to rescue a captured relative; *Josanie's War: A Chiricahua Apache Novel* is about the last Apache rising in 1885; *Aurora Crossing: A Novel of the Nez Perces* is about the war of 1877 in which the Nez Perces refused white domination and sought refuge in Canada.

Schlesier's memoir has the same careful attention to detail as his other writing, but the source, its "data", is unique: his own memory, reinforced by the diary he kept as a 15-17 year old youth. With the goal of presenting a narrative that avoids any influence of subsequent scholarly research on World War II, the diary guides him to recount those searing experiences as an anti-aircraft gunner in the heavily industrialized Ruhr region of Germany, the fierceness of Allied bombing and strafing, the destruction of the cities around him; witnessing slave labor; being drawn into the infantry on the North-West European Front late in the war; digging trenches, receiving artillery fire and all the details of battle. He also describes his brief furloughs home, the books he read supplied by a librarian determined to keep him going as a student, despite his and his comrades growing disillusionment with the war. The narrative's climax occurs as the German front is overrun by the Allies. Boy soldier and his small isolated unit are captured by a lone American soldier walking across the field in a non-defensive posture toward the German trenches, telling those before him, who have their guns trained on him, to "get up, come out." The American soldier is an American Indian; the boy soldier is hugely impressed by his fearlessness, his bravery. He and his comrades, sick of the war, obey; they are taken to a farmyard, believing they have survived. But another American soldier, crazed by recent casualties of comrades, begins to take revenge on the enemy captives. An approaching American officer intervenes. After describing a few months as a prisoner of war in France, the memoir closes as he makes his way home to his parents, who are overjoyed to have their only son back safely. A brief epilogue summarily notes that he finished high school, went on to get a PhD in anthropology from the University of Bonn; received a post-doctoral fellowship to the University of Chicago, studied "action anthropology" with Sol Tax and went on to direct one of the more successful long-term action anthropology projects with the Southern Cheyenne traditionalists. For the duration of his long career he helps them with legal arrangements that assure their legitimacy vis-à-vis the tribal council and the US government, and supports them in their struggle for cultural survival.

I have known Professor Schlesier for 50 years, and we have been together recently regarding this memoir. There is something enduring and poignant about it as written; it is like a primary source, a clinical transcription, a confession. In the words of recent anthropological writing, it is an "auto-ethnography," an account of an author's own experience within the context of a larger event or cultural setting. Rather than being a script that can be endlessly edited and manipulated for a publication, it has a certain inviolability. Upon reading Schlesier's memoir I suggested, and he endorsed, the idea of a document that would situate his wartime experiences, as presented in the memoir, within an anthropological framework. I recognized in the memoir several themes that have shown up frequently in anthropological writing on violence, trauma, and memory. When he asked me to do this, I willingly consented. This afterword therefore offers three framing ideas that situate the memoir within anthropological scholarship, at the same time demonstrating that anthropologists are human beings whose priorities and judgments are shaped by their experiences.

Survival and a life. Although Schlesier, with the help of a diary, adheres fairly strictly to the self-imposed discipline of recreating his boyhood soldier experiences as they occurred in 1943-45, "uninfluenced by objective historical scholarship...", readers may ask if this is really possible, or what other factors may have shaped the memory of events during and just after World War II. One of the most influential factors that has shaped his memory is surely the relationship of his survival to his career. Only in recent years has he even begun to talk about his war survival, and still today this is accompanied by palpable agitation and self-consciousness.

Those of us who know Karl well understand the intimate connection between the events of the war, especially his survival at the end, and in his decision to commit himself to serving the Native American community in some way as an anthropologist. But he is too modest to shout this connection from the rooftops. It is very personal for him. Recently he related to me that even the Cheyenne priests who helped him with his vision prior to signing the action anthropology contract with him only realized later, when they were together on Bear Butte Mountain in South Dakota, a sacred site for the Cheyenne, that his war experience was a strong motive in his desire to work with them.

Yet it is my distinct impression that the years of his professional career and his work with the Cheyenne have shaped his memory of that moment. The moment of his rescue is, narratively or rhetorically speaking, the pivot of the memoir. Several of my family members who read the memoir thought that this connection was the main point of the memoir. Schlesier himself speaks of "coincidences" surrounding his survival. In any event, it is the climax of his war experience as well as the beginning of the rest of his life and career. It is the cathartic moment of the memoir that juxtaposes the immanent threat of death with double rescues. The ineluctable logic of the moment requires that the life saved so dramatically is not lightly lived out. This association of a searing moment's experience to an entire life reminds me a lot of the testimony of the Rwandan genocide survivor Bugingo. Recounting his narrow escapes with death produced great agitation, as well as the need to situate these moments within the narrative of his entire life thus far.[1]

Testimony and trauma. The association of testimony to trauma is a further dimension that may be lifted out in the memoir, with the ample assistance by Schlesier who, repeatedly, alludes to the failure of words in a situation of perplexity, shock, and deep sadness. On seeing their first destruction of a German city from the train, " ... the rest of us stood rather frozen, hiding emotions ...." or, on seeing bomb damage in Wuppertal, a neighboring city, "seeing this numbed us ... we spoke little after that;" or, again, on seeing totally destroyed Wuppertal, " ... slowly the horror of it seeped into our minds. We spoke little that evening ... we were tired, physically and emotionally." And as the surrounding cities of the Ruhr were reduced to rubble by Allied bombing, "fear gripped me as it had last night.

1 John M. & Reinhild Janzen, *Do I still have a life? Voices from the aftermath of war in Rwanda and Burundi*. Lawrence, KS: University of Kansas Monographs in Anthropology, 2000.

I tried to shake it off but could not;" and "watching in silence as the red glows on the horizon or close by painted the clouds, caused an unspeakable sorrow in the heart." Again, while trudging to their anti-aircraft battery post, "we did not speak." What is the full depth of this failure of speech? How does it play itself out? Later on, the repeated confrontation with horror, terror, and the blasts of bombs, and of anti-aircraft guns, took their toll: "We had become numb to disasters, apathetic, locking our feelings away..." "I suppose I was in shock..." seems a glib way of stating an enormous emotional condition leading to an overwhelming sense of helplessness: "there was nothing we could do."

One of the insights of anthropological studies of war experience is that this paralysis of words is accompanied by the internalization of impressions deeper into one's psychic and physical being. The memory of the experience becomes embodied; it lives on in semi-conscious ways to be aroused by association with a similar sensation.

Schlesier recounts exactly such a connection between his harrowing first experience of heavy artillery fire, and reflexively reliving the experience years later when he walked by a party where fireworks were going off. Despite being dressed in suit and tie, he impulsively dove for cover. Veena Das describes the traumatic impact of violent attacks, rape of women, killing, flight, and being forced to make a new life upon thousands of individuals and families of the partition of India and Pakistan at the close of British colonialism. She also describes the violence against Sikhs in the aftermath of the assassination of Indira Gandhi by a Sikh bodyguard. Although apparently her own family, and she personally, were not directly affected, as an Indian anthropologist she understands that there is no healing, no ending of the internalized trauma. Rather, the "violence descends into the ordinary," it becomes "everyday."[2] Certain particularly painful aspects, like the rape of women, is collectively suppressed. For Sri Lankan anthropologist E. Valentine Daniel, the internalized violence of the civil war in his home country is closer, in that he is Tamil on one side of his parentage, Sinhalese on the other. His relatives carry the embodied memories of torture and violence.[3] Here too particularly intentional violence induces deeply seated fear that can only be

2 Veena Das, *Life and Words: Violence and the Descent into the Ordinary.* Berkley and Los Angeles: University of California Press, 2007.

3 E. Valentine Daniel, *Charred Lullabies: Chapters in an Anthropography of Violence.* Princeton: Princeton University Press 1996.

spoken about with difficulty. Some of his interviewees sat quietly for long periods of time before they could bring themselves to relate their experience.

Schlesier illustrates a number of the themes of these two anthropological studies of memory of violence and trauma. Like their insights to their national narrative on societal wide traumatic experience, he provides an insight into an entire category of World War II "victims" whom he has called the silent generation of boy soldiers. Similar, yet more poignant, is his first person singular ethnographic pen writing, buttressed by his diary, about his own personal experience.

Preserving sanity in the face of war's chaos. This book offers a fascinating record of Schlesier' s emotional register as the war moved toward its climax. He notes the growing nihilism in his unit, "we believed in nothing anymore." On the other hand, as still "kid[s], sometimes serious, sometimes playful, [we were] able to switch from one emotion to the other, not really knowing ..." This emotional quavering led most of his unit to volunteer for one-man torpedo suicide missions, a program that thankfully did not materialize. Reflecting on their embrace of this way out of their situation, Schlesier comments that "we were all seriously messed up." These comments are eerily similar to those collected in recent ethnographies of child soldiers, forced into service in many recent wars because of their pliability.[4] This impact of war on moral sanity was apparently not a strange thing to Schlesier even as he entered his service. He recalls a World War I veteran having told him that the war had been a "trauma for all who had been there ... " accompanied by a descending helplessness, "a mood, a feeling that what was happening was inevitable, beyond anyone's power to change ..."

Yet Schlesier appears to have been blessed more than most of his peers with support and strong role models to keep him going in the midst of the moral and emotional chaos of war. He corresponded regularly with his parents, they were the only parents who came to visit one of the boy soldiers at Sagan barracks. He had home leaves. Most remarkable was the librarian who kept him supplied with books, some even banned by the Nazi regime. His grandmother, the librarian, his parents, all nurtured his development as a scholar and human being. He mentions the memory of his grandfather, a trade-union leader, as a thread of hope and stability that kept him going in the midst of disillusionment with the

4 See for example, Alcinda Honwana, *Child Soldiers in Africa*. Philadelphia: University of Pennsylvania Press, 2005. The importance of this issue in reviewing Schlesier's Memoir was suggested to me by Marike S. Janzen, Ph.D, personal communication. June 15, 2010.

Nazi government and war machine. He was not drawn to false hopes of a secret weapon that would rescue the German war effort from defeat. Nor did he, like others, embrace the NS ideology, relish their brown shirts, or become brutal.

Schlesier's ambivalence toward the war so many years later harbors both the boyhood glorification of powerful guns and their bravery in defending their cities and communities from an enemy, as well as a memory of deep skepticism of the Nazi regime's claims and ideologies. He records glimpses of the horrors we associate with the Nazi war machine, such as the slave labor in a factory his unit protected for a time; but he also says he did not know the full horrors of their war program.

From Flakhelfer to Grenadier harbors philosophical elements conveyed by the words 'Truth", "Witnessing", and "Redemption". Truth is what he seeks, and what keeps him going. Schlesier's effort to write it the way it happened is a psychological defense against the sometimes automatic charge that all Germans bear the blame of the Holocaust.[5] The reader should be able to judge whether Schlesier's account is "true", and what this truth reveals. Witnessing is what he is doing with the memoir; his experience and his understanding of the Nazi world is what he is reporting, like it was on the inside, from the perspective of a youth who did not have knowledge of the whole. Yet he did have his suspicions. Redemption is a fitting notion to describe Schlesier's decision to dedicate his life to working with, helping, the people of the individual who saved his life. He finds redemption in scholarship, but especially in his devotion to action anthropology.

5 Daniel J. Goldhagen, *Hitler's Willing Executioners: Ordinary Germans and the Holocaust.* New York: Knopf 1996.

Further Reading

Because this memoir is based on the author's diary notes from June 10 1943 to March 19 1945, little if anything of the volumes of historical information is considered here. Dates in my diary of air raids on specific cities during the time covered could be compared with RAF and USAF records and would be found accurate. For readers who would like suggestions for further reading, a brief list is entered below.

Bacque, James. *Other Losses*. New York: St. Martin's Press 1991.

Bishop, Chris and Adam Warner. *German Weapons of World War II*. Edison, New Jersey: Chatwell Books, 2001.

Boiten, Theo. Nachtjagd. *The Night Fighter versus Bomber War over the Third Reich 1939-45*. Marlborough, England: Crowood Press, 1997.

Boiten, Theo and Martin Bowman. *Battles with the Luftwaffe. The Bomber Campaign against Germany 1942-45*. London: HarperCollins, 2001.

Grayling, A.C. *Among the Dead Cities*. New York: Walker & Company, 2006.

Friedrich, Jörg. *The Fire*. New York: Columbia University Press, 2006.

Knopp, Guido. *Die Gefangenen*. München: Bertelsmann Verlag, 2003.

Kucklick, Christoph. *Feuersturm. Der Bombenkrieg gegen Deutschland*. Hamburg: GEO Ellert & Richter Verlag, 2003.

LeTissier, Tony. *Death was our Companion*. Stroud, England: Sutton, 2003.

Lowe, Keith. *Inferno*. New York: Scribner, 2007.

MacDonogh, Giles. *After the Reich*. New York: Basic Books, 2007.

Tewes, Ludger. *Jugend im Krieg*. Essen: Reimar Hobbing Verlag 1989.